By What Authority?

Luke Gives Jesus Public Voice

MATRIX
The Bible in Mediterranean Context

EDITORIAL BOARD

John H. Elliott†   John S. Kloppenborg
Anselm Hagedorn   Douglas E. Oakman
K. C. Hanson   Gary Stansell

PREVIOUSLY PUBLISHED VOLUMES

Richard L. Rohrbaugh
The New Testament and Social-Science Criticism

Markus Cromhout
Jesus and Identity

Pieter F. Craffert
The Life of a Galilean Shaman

Douglas E. Oakman
Jesus and the Peasants

Stuart L. Love
Jesus and the Marginal Women

Eric C. Stewart
Gathered around Jesus

Dennis C. Duling
A Marginal Scribe

Jason Lamoreaux
Ritual, Women, and Philippi

Ernest Van Eck
The Parables of Jesus the Galilean

Bruce J. Malina and John J. Pilch
Handbook of Biblical Social Values (3rd ed.)

K. C. Richardson
Early Christian Care for the Poor

Douglas E. Oakman
The Radical Jesus, the Bible, and the Great Transformation

By What Authority?

Luke Gives Jesus Public Voice

JEROME H. NEYREY, SJ

 CASCADE *Books* • Eugene, Oregon

BY WHAT AUTHORITY?
Luke Gives Jesus Public Voice

Matrix: The Bible in Mediterranean Context 13

Copyright © 2021 Jerome H. Neyrey, SJ. All rights reserved. Except for brief quotations in critical publications or reviews, no part of this book may be reproduced in any manner without prior written permission from the publisher. Write: Permissions, Wipf and Stock Publishers, 199 W. 8th Ave., Suite 3, Eugene, OR 97401.

Cascade Books
An Imprint of Wipf and Stock Publishers
199 W. 8th Ave., Suite 3
Eugene, OR 97401

www.wipfandstock.com

PAPERBACK ISBN: 978-1-7252-9332-8
HARDCOVER ISBN: 978-1-7252-9333-5
EBOOK ISBN: 978-1-7252-9334-2

Cataloguing-in-Publication data:

Names: Neyrey, Jerome H., SJ, author.
Title: By what authority? : Luke gives Jesus public voice / Jerome H. Neyrey, SJ.
Description: Eugene, OR: Cascade Books, 2021. | Matrix: The Bible in Mediterranean Context 13. | Includes bibliographical references and indexes.
Identifiers: ISBN: 978-1-7252-9332-8 (paperback). | ISBN: 978-1-7252-9333-5 (hardcover). | ISBN: 978-1-7252-9334-2 (ebook).
Subjects: LCSH: Jesus Christ—Person and offices. | Bible. Luke—Criticism, interpretation, etc. | Bible. Luke—Social scientific criticism. | Bible—Luke 1,1–4—Criticism, interpretation, etc. | New Testament—Language, style. | Rhetoric in the Bible.
Classification: BS2555.6.P67 N49 2021 (print). | BS2555.6.P67 (ebook).

Unless otherwise noted, Scripture quotations are taken from the New Revised Standard Version Bible, copyright © 1989 National Council of the Churches of Christ in the United States of America. Used by permission. All rights reserved worldwide.

Scripture quotations marked (RSV) re taken from the Revised Standard Version Bible © 1946, 1952, and 1971 National Council of the Churches of Christ in the United States of America. Used by permission. All rights reserved worldwide.

To all past and present members of
the Context Group,
who continually educated me
to understand the cultural world of Jesus

Contents

Acknowledgments | ix
Abbreviations | xi

Introduction: Topic, Plan, and Purpose | 1

PART 1: Reading Luke with Social-Science Lenses

1. Reading an Ancient Writing through Modern Lenses | 7
2. Jesus in Social Science Perspective | 32
3. An Ethos for Jesus via Status-Elevation Rituals | 42
4. Confirming Jesus's Roles and Status with Ceremonies | 54

PART 2: Reading Luke with Rhetorical Lenses

5. How Beginnings Begin | 77
6. Making a Rhetorical Ethos for Jesus | 100
7. Luke's Own Ethos (1:1–4) | 110

Bibliography | 133
Index of Subjects | 143
Index of Scripture | 147

Acknowledgments

During the pandemic,
access to library materials and services
became difficult.
Praise and gratitude to
Dr. Martha Allen of St. Louis University
for providing what was available,
and always with good humor.

Gratitude to Vincent Orlando, S. J.
who rescued this manuscript
from many faults
by his careful reading.

Abbreviations

Ancient Sources

Ant.	Josephus, *Antiquities*
De Inv.	Cicero, *De Inventione rhetorica*. Translated by H. M. Hubble. LCL. Cambridge: Harvard University Press, 1960
De Orat.	Cicero, *De Oratore*. Edited and translated by E. W. Sutton and H. Rackham. LCL. Cambridge: Harvard University Press, 1942
Epam.	Nepos, *De Viris Illustribus, Epamonidas*. Translated by John C. Rolfe. LCL. Cambridge: Harvard University Press, 1984
Hist.	Thucydides, *History*
Inst. Orat.	Quintilian, *Institutio Oratoriae*. Translated by Donald Russell. LCL. Cambridge: Harvard University Press, 2001
Mem.	Xenophon, *Memorabilia*. Translated by E. C. Marchant. LCL. Cambridge: Harvard University Press, 1918
Menex.	Plato, *Menexenus*. Translated by N. R. M. Lamb. LCL. Cambridge: Harvard University Press, 1969
Mor.	Plutarch, *Moralia*. Translated by Frank Cole Babbitt. LCL. Cambridge: Harvard University Press, 1949

Rhet.	Aristotle, *The Art of Rhetoric*. Translated by John Henry Freese. Aristotle in 23 volumes 22. LCL. Cambridge: Harvard University Press, 1975
Rhet. ad Her.	Cicero, *Rhetorica ad Herennium*. Translated by Harry Caplan. LCL. Cambridge: Harvard University Press, 1954
Top.	Cicero, *Topica*. Translated by H. M. Hubble. LCL. Cambridge: Harvard University Press, 1960

Modern Sources

ABD	*Anchor Bible Dictionary*. Edited by David Noel Freedman. 6 vols. New York: Doubleday, 1992
ANRW	*Aufstieg und Niedergang der römischen Welt*
ATR	*Anglican Theological Review*
BBR	*Bulletin for Biblical Research*
BibIntSer	Biblical Interpretation Series
BDAG	Frederick W. Danker, Walter Bauer, William Arndt, and F. Wilbur Gingrich. *Greek-English Lexicon of the New Testament and Other Early Christian Literature*. 3rd ed. Chicago: University of Chicago Press, 2000
Bib	*Biblica*
BJS	Brown Judaic Studies
BTB	*Biblical Theology Bulletin*
BR	*Biblical Research*
BZ	*Biblische Zeitschrift*
CBQ	*Catholic Biblical Quarterly*
ConNT	Coniectanea Novi Testamenti
CQ	*Classical Quarterly*
CW	*Classical World*
DR	*Downside Review*

Abbreviations

EvQ	*Evangelical Quarterly*
GRBS	*Greek, Roman, and Byzantine Studies*
HTR	*Harvard Theological Review*
HUCA	*Hebrew Uniion College Annual*
HvTSt	*Hervormde teologiese studies*
Int	*Interpretation*
JAAR	*Journal of the American Academy of Religion*
JBL	*Journal of Biblical Literature*
JHS	*Journal of Hellenic Studies*
JJS	*Journal of Jewish Studies*
JSJ	*Journal for the Study of Judaism in the Persian, Hellenistic, and Roman Period*
JSNT	*Journal for the Study of the New Testament*
JTS	*Journal of Theological Studies*
LCL	Loeb Classical Library
LNTS	Library of New Testament Studies
NovT	*Novum Testamentum*
NTS	*New Testament Studies*
PRSt	*Perspectives in Religious Studies*
RB	*Revue Biblique*
RSR	*Reserches de science religieuse*
SANT	Studien zum Alten und Neuen Testaments
SBLDS	Society of Biblical Literature Dissertation Series
SBLSP	Society of Biblical Literature Seminar Papers
SNTSMS	Society for New Testament Studies Monograph Series
SP	Sacra Pagina
ST	*Studia Theologica*
TAPA	*Transactions and Proceedings of the American Philological Association*

Abbreviations

TDNT	*Theological Dictionary of the New Testament.* 10 vols. Edited by Gerhard Kittel and Gerhard Friedrich. Translated by Geoffrey W. Bromiley. Grand Rapids: Eerdmans, 1964–1976
WGRW	Writings from the Greco-Roman World
ZAW	*Zeitschrift fur die altestamentliche Wissenschaft*
ZNW	*Zeitschrift fur die neutestamentliche Wissenschaft*

Introduction
Topic, Plan, and Purpose

"By what authority you do these things,
or who gave you this authority?" (Luke 20:2)

As Jesus begins to act in public, Luke narrates a similar scene three times:

4:15 He began to *teach* in their *synagogues* and was praised by everyone.

4:16 He went to the *synagogue* on the sabbath day, as was his custom. He stood up to *read* . . .

4:31 He went down to Capernaum . . . and was *teaching* them on the sabbath.

WHAT DOES THIS *PUBLIC voice* mean? It describes speaking in a public place, either a village agora or a synagogue. "Speaking" means teaching with authority. We ask how and why Luke suddenly credits Jesus with public voice and expects his audience to approve of this. By public voice we mean this:

> Public speaking (also called oratory or oration) is the process or act of performing a speech to a live audience. Public speaking is commonly understood as formal, face-to-face speaking of a single person to a group of listeners. Traditionally, public speaking was considered to be a part of the art of persuasion. The act can accomplish particular purposes including to inform, to persuade, and to entertain. (Wikipedia, s.v. "Public speaking")

Since Luke constructs his own gospel narrative, he is in charge of what role and status he ascribes to Jesus and how this is conveyed by whom, when, where, and why. We presume that Luke is carefully describing the person Jesus as one fit for the task, and as one whom Luke's audience would appreciate as a valid public speaker. Why can Luke expect his listeners to accept Jesus as a "teacher" in 4:15? How has he established Jesus's authority to teach and expound the Scriptures?

Yet is Luke really concerned about Jesus's "authority" to speak publicly when he narrates that Jesus began to do this? Is Luke interested in the construction of the character of Jesus as one with a right to public voice? This is not about the historical Jesus, which seems beyond our reach in this regard, but about Luke's narrative about Jesus, when "He *began to teach* in their *synagogues* and *was praised* by everyone" (4:15), and when he spoke in Nazareth's *synagogue* (4:16–30). And so, we argue this hypothesis. Although Jesus only began to speak publicly in synagogues in Luke 4:14–15, Luke had already groomed his audience to accept Jesus as deserving "public voice"—that is, he is *authorized* to speak in public venues to diverse audiences about specific topics. Thus we ask a very different question from what generally guides scholars examining Luke 1–4. In fact, we simply do not find any scholarly interest in this question at all.

To answer this, we propose several parallel avenues of inquiry. One way is to compare the way Luke presents Jesus from birth to synagogue with the way Mark, Matthew, and John do. If they too are interested in this topic, what can we learn from how they go about this task? Another way would be to consider the question itself by using many research methods, including social-science concepts and models, which offer new paths of inquiry. For example, persons in Jesus's culture were collectivists or group-oriented, not individualists such as we are. The premiere value in their culture was honor (respect, standing), which presumes that an audience knew what honor (role, status) Jesus enjoyed and how he came by it. We, however, must learn this value and its choreography. Moreover, since Jesus performs verbally, it would greatly help if we could examine the narrative in terms of communication modeling (who says what to whom, when, and why). Are there status-transformation rituals that signal to Luke's audience that someone is ascribing to Jesus this public role?

Still another mode of inquiry is available, namely, considering the rhetoric employed by Luke to convince his audience that Jesus is worthy to speak and that they should listen. This requires that we consult the common

Introduction

rhetorical handbooks from Aristotle to Quintilian so as to investigate how orators were instructed to compose speeches and writers to write prose. And so, we must examine the rhetorical materials that instruct orators in terms of the sequence of parts of a composition, in this case knowing what belongs in a proper exordium. For example, does this rhetoric instruct us to see how Luke constructed an ethos for Jesus as part of his exordium? Moreover, when *bioi* were composed, what conventional topics were typically treated to honor a person. This brings us into conversation with conventional rhetorical genres, such as *encomium*, *chreia*, and *syncrisis*. Without knowledge of these rhetorical data, it is difficult to see how modern readers of Luke can follow the rhetorical argument Luke made when he employed conventional ways of speaking and persuading.

We argue that Luke is quite aware of making Jesus fit for public speaking, and that he begins this from the start of his narrative. He employs the rhetorical genres and forms that he was taught as a student of rhetoric, genres which he mastered and that his audience would recognize. He was not ignorant of how to write a speech, which begins with an exordium, or an encomium, which includes traditional topics such as origins, birth, significant accompanying events, and training and education.

This monograph, then, will consist of two parts. First, by viewing Luke 1:1—4:41 in terms of social-science models and concepts, we can learn the communication dynamics common to most peoples, ancient and modern. This view of Luke 1–4 makes salient the questions examined in all contemporary studies of communication, which can provide even biblical scholars with a way of hearing and reading not generally formalized, much less used, by them. Second, the bulk of this study focuses on Luke 1–4 in terms of rhetoric employed, that is, the conventional (and necessary) ways that any orator or author would go about his task, namely, the use of the common rhetorical ways of gathering data and expressing them in forms and genres known by ancient listeners and expected by them. Luke, who was educated according the rhetorical handbooks called *progymnasmata*, learned the basic but conventional ways of communicating to an ancient audience. This includes knowledge of the parts of a work (exordium, narration, and so forth), the contents of a proper ethos (knowledge, virtue, and goodwill), and the encomiastic ways of creating an ethos (origins, nurture and training, deeds of virtue).

Our aim in approaching Luke 1–4 in all of these various ways remains the simple inquiry about how Luke prepared his audience so that Jesus, at about thirty years old, could immediately exercise public voice. And the way Luke went about his project necessarily requires that we enter his cultural world to learn what ways of expression existed and were possible.

PART 1

*Reading Luke
with Social-Science Lenses*

CHAPTER 1

Reading an Ancient Writing through Modern Lenses

> Without... theory, it is impossible to know what to look for... the relevance of evidence depends upon the theory which is dominating the discussion.
>
> —Alfred North Whitehead[1]

> The difficulty is that without interpretation [i.e., theory] there are no facts. Every observation entails a point of view, a set of connections. The pure empiricist would drown in meaningless impressions. Even so simple a task as translating a sentence from an ancient language into our own requires some sense of the social matrices of both the original utterance and ourselves...To collect facts without any theory too often means to substitute for theory our putative common sense. Making that substitution modernizes no less than does the scientist who follows his theory, for our common sense, too, is a cultural artifact.
>
> —Wayne A. Meeks[2]

T0 DISCOVER HOW LUKE makes Jesus worthy to have public voice, we propose reading his narrative employing four modern ways of understanding how this might be done: (1) employing communication modeling, (2) categorizing types of persons in antiquity, (3) appreciating honor, the premiere social value of that culture, and (4) plotting Luke's narrative

---

1. Quoted in LeClerc, *Whitehead's Metaphysics*, 45.
2. Meeks, *The First Urban Christians*, 5.

by means of rituals and ceremonies. We begin with these social-scientific approaches because simply reading Luke once more without a particular question or a distinctive mode of reading has little prospect of yielding more than has already been written.[3] But in this monograph we are urging that new questions be asked based on different ways of reading with, perhaps, different results. But what are these new ways of reading, and what is their pedigree? Why employ them? What might they tell us? Are they necessary?

Without fresh perspectives on typical modes of communication, we would be wasting a lot of time and effort. Yet novelty for its own sake does not warrant that we spend time and effort needlessly. We are, however, doing nothing more here than our peers in the science of communication have proposed, which we now use with their guidance. Moreover, the very model of communication from the social sciences is itself based on widespread cultural investigations ancient and modern and can help us escape thinking about ancient persons in an anachronistic and ethnocentric way.

Communication Modeling

All modern textbooks on communication contain an independent chapter on "communication," by means of which scholars identify the regular elements in all communication.[4] This means that they isolate and identify **Who** says **What** to **Whom**, via **what Channel/Mediator**, for **what Purpose**. Inasmuch as Jesus does not have public voice until Luke 4:14–15, Luke's audience must pay attention to what others say about him and for

---

3. We start with social-science models because it is no longer legitimate to presume that modern readers can have an "immaculate perception" of materials from a culture centuries removed from us. To escape anachronism and ethnocentricity, readers are urged to approach an ancient author such as Luke and his culturally different prose narrative aware of the radical differences between us and them. Social-science models equip us to appreciate precisely how "they" wrote and spoke, which is generally opaque to "us." Cultural models can school us to be aware in very specific ways how something like "public speaking" would be understood then, not now. We are not, then, imposing any model on Luke and his narrative, but schooling ourselves to see what elements generally go into communication, and to recognize what they would look like when dressed in their proper cultural robes.

4. All introductory handbooks on communication begin with a section on "Communication Theory." Currently there is widespread agreement about the contents, shape, and flow of this model. We choose one representative, Rothwell, *In the Company of Others*, 7–17; see also Berlo, *The Process of Communication*, 47–60.

what purpose.⁵ As we shall see, Luke narrates that it takes "thirty years" or so completely to build the foundation for Jesus himself to begin his own communication. But the project began much earlier.

Jesus himself counsels disciples to plan ahead before beginning an enterprise (Luke 14:28–32), and so should we. What are we doing when we examine Luke 1–4 in terms of communication theory? What hypothesis do we have about this endeavor? We begin by dividing the narrative into three parts: first, Jesus's infancy/childhood, then his appearance with John at the Jordan, and finally Jesus' mature "teaching" in the synagogue. We expect that at each stage there is formal communication about the role and status of Jesus, which is made by persons with attested authority to speak about him. From the start, the communication about Jesus functions to build a foundation, then a structure, and finally a stage authorizing Jesus to have public voice, that is, a proper ethos. These communications, moreover, are intended to inform a widening narrative public about Jesus, affirming his right to speak publicly.

And so, in this process we are taught how to think about Jesus as his heavenly communicator would have us do. We anticipate that (1) the ultimate **Sender/Speaker** (**Who** speaks?) will always be God, and that (2) this **Sender-of-Senders** speaks **through Channels/Mediators**, such as angels and prophets, (3) to **Recipients**, the first hearers, (4) a **gospel message**, i.e. always about Jesus, (5) calibrated for **every stage of Jesus's life** (preconception, birth, infancy) and (6) **for the Purpose** of authorizing Jesus eventually to have public voice. Thus, Luke's overall rhetorical strategy in chapters 1–4 argues that from 1:5 Jesus was regularly attested to have certain roles and statuses that authorize him for a public role. And so, his authority was not something that came to him only as an adult but has been ascribed to him from the beginning. In this chapter only statements spoken by narrative characters about Jesus are discussed, not narrative details, that is, information provided by the author. Luke indeed communicates through narration

---

5. In his commentary on Luke, Mikeal C. Parsons (*Luke*, 3) offers a version of this model: "To orient the user of this commentary, it is helpful to speak of the now familiar relationship among author, text, and audience, adjusted here to account for the particular shape of composition and reception of ancient texts."

Model of Communication for Reading Ancient Literature
Author(s) ➔ Scribe(s) ➔ Text ➔ Audience

He intends his model to recognize advancements made in understanding ancient texts with recognition of modern concerns, such as "reader" or "lector" and "authorial audience," and other specifications, like "implied author" and "implied reader," and the like.

of events, but here we focus only on what certain characters actually say about Jesus. The conventional template for communication modeling identifies these significant elements. Although repetitious, these categories alert us to attend to (1) the **Sender**, (2) the **recipients**, (3) the **channel** or **mediator**, (4) the **message**, and (5)the **purpose** of the communication.[6]

What Is Said about Jesus, Babe and Infant?

Luke 1:30–36

The **Sender**, God, employs an angelic **channel**, the angel Gabriel. The **recipient**, Mary, is immediately declared honorable in God's eyes, thus worthy of this **message**: "You have found favor with God" (1:30). **When** and **where** this occurs impact the importance of the **what** is said: (1) "in the sixth month," a link to the conception of John; (2) in "Nazareth of Galilee," an insignificant village far away from the urban world of Jerusalem and its temple; (3) "to a virgin [merely] betrothed to a man whose name was Joseph."[7] Furthermore, the **channel**, Gabriel, speaks a strange **message** to this young female **recipient**: "You will conceive in your womb and bear a son, and you will name him Jesus": you are to bear a son, but not by Joseph, your espoused. The angel's **message**, moreover, speaks to the honorable role and status of this son: "He will be great, and will be called the Son of the Most High, and the Lord God will give to him the throne of his ancestor David" (1:32). Thus, God ascribes to the forthcoming son the eminent role of "king," not just any successor of David, but one "of whose kingdom there will be no end" (1:33). This **message**, therefore, ascribes maximum status

---

6. This model of communication has been fully displayed in the fifth edition of a popular textbook: O'Hair et al., *A Speaker's Guidebook*, 13–15. Their model includes the following elements: (1) source/sender; (2) encoding the message: converting thoughts into words; (3) receiver (who decodes message); (4) message (content of the communication process: thoughts and ideas put into meaningful expressions); (5) channel: medium through which speaker delivers a message; (6) shared meaning: the mutual understanding of a message between speaker and audience; (7) rhetorical situation: the situation that created the need for it in the first place; and (8) audience-centered approach: keeping the needs, values, attitudes, and wants of listeners firmly in focus; (9) speech purpose: what you want the audience to learn or do or believe as a result of your speech. For the sake of this study, we prefer the briefer one proposed by Rothwell.

7. Although we concentrate on the communication between **Sender** and **recipient**, others accurately observe a literary form in which the whole episode is cast, namely, a commissioning form; see Brown, "Luke's Method."

and role to the son/king, a public role. Its **purpose** implies that prophecies now being fulfilled indicate that God is inaugurating a kingdom that will have no end.[8]

The **message**, however, itself creates a problem, immediately recognized by the **recipient**: "How can this be, since I am a virgin?" (1:34). Thus, a second **message** is needed to tell the **recipient** how the **Sender** will solve this problem: "The Holy Spirit will come upon you, and the power of the Most High will overshadow you" (1:35). This extends the grant of honor by God: "The child to be born will be *holy*; he will be called *Son of God*." Furthermore, this communication is supported by a "sign," i.e. proof, which attests to its veracity: "Elizabeth has conceived a son . . . this is the sixth month for her who was said to be barren" (1:36).

It is never wise to take for granted what Luke intended when he called the pregnancy of Elizabeth a "sign." While we are familiar with the phrase "signs and wonders," these Lukan "signs" are quite different. True, "signs and wonders" speak about God's past powerful actions, especially in regard to Israel's liberation from Egypt (Exod 7:3; Deut 4:34; Pss 78:43; 105:27; and Acts 7:36). "Signs" in the Old Testament, however, are not self-explanatory, and always require an interpretation. But, in the New Testament, while they may be portents of future events (Matt 24:24; Mark 13:22), they frequently serve as evidence for and confirmation of Jesus's role and status (John 2:11, 23). The term "sign" most frequently serves as credentials, especially for Jesus (Acts 2:22), but also for the apostles (Acts 2:43; 4:16). Thus, the mention of "signs and wonders" serves as testimony about God's benevolence, and so constitutes part of God's honor claim. They testify to God's power and patronage, and should be understood in terms of the pivotal cultural value in antiquity, honor.

Luke, however, uses "sign" in a more rhetorical way, namely, as "proof" of something. Zechariah's silence is "proof" that he had a vision; Mary is given "proof" that "nothing is impossible with God" with the announcement that Elizabeth, once barren, has conceived. Likewise, the shepherds are given a "sign" that confirms the angelic announcement: "This will be a sign for you: you will find a child wrapped in bands of cloth and lying in a manger" (2:12). Thus, in functional terms, these three remarks invite consideration as "proofs" in a rhetorical argument.

---

8. Frequently in communication modeling, attention is given to the **medium** of the communication, such as incense or music. Parsons has argued that the **medium** of communication here is a "dream vision" (*Luke*, 33–40); for material on "dream visions," see Dobson, *Reading Dreams*; and J. Hanson, "Dreams and Visions."

By What Authority?

Aristotle discusses "proofs" (*pisteis*), distinguishing between artificial and nonartificial ones. By the former he means "all those which have not been furnished by ourselves, but were already in existence . . . by the latter, all that can be constructed by system and by our own efforts" (*Rhet.*1.2.2). Inartificial proofs, such as witnesses and contracts, speak for themselves or stand alone. But artificial proofs need to be constructed so that they prove this but not that. Later on, Aristotle discusses how to make an argument, distinguishing two kinds, "induction" and "syllogism" (1.2.8). Continuing, he states that "the example (*paradeigma*) is induction," whereas "the enthymeme [is] a syllogism" (1.2.8). Both "example" and "enthymeme" are "concerned with things which may be other than they are, the "example" being a kind of induction and the "enthymeme" a kind of syllogism. "For if one of these is well known, there is no need to mention it." He then considers what must be a "necessary result," which makes something into a secure argument. Accordingly, Zechariah's muteness can be understood as an inartificial "proof," which makes sense when considered as an enthymeme. His delay in the temple and his subsequent muteness were *proof* of something specific to those awaiting him: "They perceived that he had seen a vision in the temple" (1:22). This exemplifies an enthymeme syllogism, even though only two parts of the syllogism are present. Ideally the argument would go as such: All priests who stay in the temple offering incense and exit radically changed have seen a vision; Zechariah stayed and exited mute; therefore, Zechariah saw a vision. The premise that "all priests who stay . . . and exit changed" is not stated. This is a "sign," but in our low-context culture (where many things are assumed to be unknown until they are explained to the audience) it needs an explanation in order to become an argument. In Luke's culture (a high-context culture, where many things are assumed to be known without having to be explained to the audience) the sign does not need to be accompanied by an explanation in order to become an argument.

Gabriel declares that with the **Sender** (God) "nothing is impossible" (1:37). What the **Sender** says is true and will come to pass; for this **Sender** can affect the outcome of his **message**. Fittingly, this **message** is received by the **recipient** with the cultural virtue proper to ancient females: "Here am I, the servant of the Lord; let it be with me according to your word" (1:38). Therefore, God speaks through his channel, Gabriel, a message of an extraordinary grant of honor to the forthcoming son. Put another way, God himself is creating the proper ethos for Jesus, and this before he was born.

Jesus, therefore, is ascribed an exceptional role and status by a person who ascribes all honor, especially this.

Luke 2:11–18

Luke narrates a communication between the honorable heavenly world and earth's meanest recipients. God, of course, the **Ultimate Sender**, sends his **channel** (angels, again), to unlikely **recipients** (again), at an appropriate time and place: (1) **when** = the very night of the birth, and (2) **where** = in the fields where shepherds tended their flocks. The **message** is incredibly amazing: "Good news of great joy for all the people . . . to you is born this day in the city of David a Savior, who is the Anointed, the Lord" (2:10–11). In confirmation of this **message**, "a multitude of the heavenly host praise God," the **Source** of the **Message**: "Glory to God in the highest heaven, and on earth peace among those whom he favors!" (2:13–14). Again a "sign" attesting to its veracity is given, albeit a strange sign (2:12). Homer Giblin wrote an important study on this sign. He concluded that the manger is "the sign of God's being the sustenance of his people . . . the sign is less an indication of the child's nature than of his function in revealing God's new rapport with his people. The main scope of the text is theocentric rather than *Christocentric*."[9] Giblin's argument supports the claim that God is the **Sender-of-Senders**, who uses angelic **channels** to speak a **message**, by the **medium** of a "sign." Obviously, the **recipients** have ears to hear, and so "they went with haste and found Mary and Joseph, and the child lying in the manger" (2:16). But communication continues as the original **recipients** themselves become **channels** of this **message**, which should be called a "gospel," not just news: "They made known what had been told them about this child" (2:17). And success attends their communication: "All who heard it were amazed at what the shepherds told them" (2:18).

Once more, God **speaks** through a **channel** to unlikely **recipients** a **message** of maximum significance, which is intended to spread abroad. The **message**, about Jesus, ascribes to him a significant role and status, "a Savior, who is the Anointed, the Lord" (2:11). But this "Savior" is a mere newborn.[10] Now the **purpose** becomes clearer: the message given the shepherds is intended for many other recipients, namely, Israel; thus, it should

---

9. Giblin, "Reflections on the Sign of the Manger," 100–101.

10. Luke carefully discriminates stages in Jesus' life. See Golden, "'Pais,' 'Child,' and 'Slave,'" 93; and Saburin, "The Growing of Christ," 23.

intentionally expand beyond the first recipients as a gospel to be told again and again. If Luke's audience and nameless people in Luke's Gospel wonder about John the Baptist, "What then will this child become?" (1:66), no doubt Luke expects his audience to appreciate all the more the superior ethos he is making for Jesus.

Luke 2:25–38

Whereas God sent angelic messengers earlier, the **Sender's** Spirit prompts two prophets, male and female, to speak a **message** about the child. The **Sender**, who is God, acts now through another heavenly **channel**, who functions three times in this communication: "the Holy Spirit rested on him ... it had been revealed to him by the Holy Spirit ... and guided by the Spirit" (2:25–27). Simeon, the **recipient**, comes to the temple because of "Spirit" communication he received, which establishes his role as a prophet. Moreover, he is a trustworthy person, deserving of respect because he "was righteous and devout, looking forward to the consolation of Israel" (2:25). Simeon's **message**, moreover, fulfils a promise spoken by God that he "would not see death before he had seen the Lord's Anointed" (2:26). This, then, is a continuation of a **message**, not something novel. In explanation of this, Simeon articulates this prior message: "my eyes have seen your salvation, which you have prepared in the presence of all peoples, a light for revelation to the Gentiles and for glory to your people Israel" (2:30–32). The **when** and **where** emphasize the message's significance: this occurs in the temple immediately after Jesus is dedicated to God. This narrative connection means that Simeon's current **message** should be understood as an explanation of the previous ritual. Luke's audience has become aware of the narrative meaning of what dedication to God implies. God's **purpose** continues to be the ascription of great honor to the infant Jesus through his prophet: "the salvation which you have prepared in the presence of all peoples" (2:30). Once more, the **message** is not just a personal favor to Simeon but is intended for all peoples: "light for revelation to the Gentiles and for glory to your people Israel" (2:32).[11] The person designated by this **message** will surely act in a public role, which is now being authorized.

---

11. Fitzmyer (*The Gospel according to Luke I–IX*, 422) observes how Simeon's oracle makes an advance over the proclamation of the angels, in that God's "salvation" is announced in the sight of all peoples, the Gentiles as well as Israel.

Luke, who loves to narrate stories in gender pairs, narrates that a female prophet balances a male one. Anna must be heard, because her credentials warrant respect: "the daughter of Phanuel, of the tribe of Asher . . . of a great age . . . a widow to the age of eighty-four. She never left the temple but worshiped there with fasting and prayer night and day" (2:37). God **sends** this prophetess a **message**, for which she acts as **channel**: "[She began to] speak about the child to all who were looking for the redemption of Jerusalem" (2:38). **When? Where?** She speaks on the same occasion as Simeon and in the same place, the temple. Moreover, she speaks while giving formal praise to God, itself a worshipful act. Both prophetic communications **function** to continue to establish the honorable role and status of the infant.

In summary, what does reading Luke's narrative through this lens tell us? Once more, God, the **Sender-of-Senders**, continuously sends a **message about Jesus**, which is of great importance, through three **channels** (Holy Spirit, Simeon, and Anna), whose ultimate **recipients** are not just the parents or the prophets but "the Gentiles" and "your people Israel." **Where** the message is given (i.e., at the temple) and **when** it is delivered (i.e., at Jesus's dedication) heighten its significance. These **messages function** to make significant honor claims for Jesus, which deserve respect because the **channels** are trustworthy figures, mandated to speak by the heavenly **Sender**. And they speak to a future public role. As noted, the construction of Jesus's ethos continually increases, the veracity of which cannot be doubted.[12] And so Theophilus's *asphaleia* (full truth) about Jesus is becoming more and more secure.

What Is Said about Jesus When "Thirty Years Old"?

Luke 3:1–17

The narrative of the relationship of John (son of Zechariah and Elizabeth) with Jesus (son of Mary and Joseph) began thirty years earlier (1:5–80). Their mothers were "kinswomen," implying some blood relationship. Their relationship is renewed when John and Jesus are mature in age. When both are "about thirty years old," a significant communication begins when John, himself an authorized prophet, comes on the scene, at a specific time and place: "The word of God came to John, son of Zechariah in the wilderness"

---

12. Saburin, "The Growing of Christ," 23.

(Luke 3:2). John himself is awarded public voice, which was prepared for three decades earlier.

All four Gospels attest that John, **channel**, witnesses to Jesus, that is, he communicates a **message** about him to the diverse crowds, **recipients**, who come to him. This, of course, begins with the **Sender-of-Senders** authorizing John. But the narrative in 3:1–17 is not totally about his communication about Jesus. John begins by "preaching a baptism of repentance for the forgiveness of sins" (3:3). When John finally speaks about Jesus, he himself does not initiate the topic, for he only responds to questioning about John himself by his audience; thus, he is prompted to speak, but not by spirit: "The people were filled with expectation, and all were questioning in their hearts concerning John, whether he might be the Messiah" (3:15). And even here, what John says proves to be significantly weaker than what angels and prophets had previously declared.

Luke prepared this scene "thirty years ago," when John was just born. If John is to speak later, he needs credentials of his own to give any **message** about Jesus. Luke narrates the foundations of this very early in his narrative. John's generational origins are of a priestly lineage (1:5): John's father was in fact serving as a priest before God. The **Sender**, God, employs an angelic **channel**, Gabriel, to deliver a **message** to a **recipient**, a village priest. **Where?** At the altar in the temple. **When?** At "the hour of incense." The **message** informs Zechariah of the special birth of a son, who will take the role of prophet rather than his father's role as a priest. The communication succeeds in one sense, but fails in another. The **recipient** does not accept the **message**: Zechariah "did not believe my words." The father fails, but the son's role and status stand firm. Moreover, at the circumcision and naming of John, Zechariah first "blessed God" (1:64 and 68) and then, "filled with the Holy Spirit, prophesied": "And you, child, will be called the prophet of the Most High; for you will go before the Lord to prepare his ways" (1:76). Zechariah mutates from **recipient** of a **message** to an authorized **channel**. Now the communication is complete: God continues as **Sender**, **channeling** (Zechariah "filled with the Holy Spirit"), with a **message** about God's fulfilling his promise by John's birth. The **recipients**, those hearing and those who later heard the **message** wonder, "What then will this child become?" (1:66). But the **message** is clear, a prophet is born. And so, the **Sender** establishes John's credentials eventually to speak about Jesus. So much for the foundations of John's ethos.

From newborn to adult, John remains offstage;[13] but at a certain **time** ("In the fifteenth year of the reign of Emperor Tiberius, when Pontius Pilate was governor of Judea") and in a certain **place** ("in the wilderness... all the region around the Jordan"), the **Sender** sends a **message** to this **recipient** ("The word of God came to John son of Zechariah," 3:2). The **message** here echoes what was prophetically spoken earlier: "Prepare the way of the Lord" (1:76), only now it comes in a formal citation of the prophet Isaiah, that is, by means of another **channel**: "Prepare the way of the Lord, make his paths straight" (3:4). The **message** articulates John's public role and status, which are essential in order for any audience to accept John's own communication about "the one who is to come" (7:19).

Finally, Luke allows John to speak about Jesus, but he does so by way of a rhetorical comparison, a syncrisis. Although the crowd's question is clear, "All were questioning in their hearts concerning John, whether he might be the Messiah" (3:15), the answer is no. We step aside from our declared intention to examine communications made by a **Sender** to **recipients**, to examine John's **message** by means of a rhetorical genre, the progymnastic comparison (syncrisis), to see what **message** is communicated by it. Many have noted the parallels between John and Jesus, which we argue are significantly more than mere parallels, but are comparisons constructed according to the rhetorical genre, syncrisis. We follow here the format used by Parsons and Martin,[14] which constructs the John-Jesus syncrisis according to the conventional encomiastic topics we will be observing shortly, that is, origins, nurture and training, pursuits and deeds, and death. Because of the scope of this book, we are examining only Luke 1 and 3. Moreover, we are both expanding and compressing the presentation by Parsons and Martin.

---

13. Much interest has been shown in some connection between John and Qumran; whatever the historicity of this turns out to be, it is unknown to Luke; see Robinson, "The Baptism of John and the Qumran Community"; Fitzmyer, *The Gospel according to Luke I-IX*, 459-60, offers a mature judgment on this: "John's baptism finds a plausible matrix in the general baptist movement known to have existed in Palestine roughly between 150 B.C. and A.D. 250. A number of Jewish and Christian groups emerged in this period that practiced some form of ritual washing. Though the forms differed and the connotations attached to them varied, the washings of the Essenes, of John and his disciples (Acts 18:25; John 3:23-25), of Jesus and his disciples (John 3:22)... are examples of this general movement."

14. Parsons and Martin, *Ancient Rhetoric and the New Testament*, 264-68.

John the Baptist	Jesus
Origins	**Origins**
• geographical: village in Judean "hill country"	• geographical: not Nazareth in Galilee, but eventually the city of David
• generational: Zechariah, priest of the division	• generational: Joseph of the house of David; Mary, tribe unspecified
• generational: Zechariah, priest of the division of Abijah; Elizabeth, a daughter of Aaron	• generational: kinship of John and Jesus confirmed: "'Your kinswoman Elizabeth has conceived a son' . . . Mary set out and went with haste to a Judean town in the hill country, where she entered the house of Zechariah and greeted Elizabeth."
• kinship of John and Jesus confirmed: Mary visits Elizabeth	
• no genealogy	
	• genealogy
Marvelous Occurrences at Birth	**Marvelous Occurrences at Birth**
• angelic pronouncement of birth	• angelic pronouncement of birth
• oracle about birth, name, and career	• oracle about birth, name, and career
• speech returned to Zechariah	• angelic proclamation about birth
• special name and role declared	• special name, given by the angel, special role (i.e., son to be dedicated to God)
Nurture and Training	**Nurture and Training**
• circumcision	• special rituals: circumcision, dedication, annual Passover pilgrimage
• "The child grew and became strong in spirit"	• "he went down with them and was obedient to them . . . Jesus increased in wisdom and in years, and in divine and human favor"
• did not take his father's role/craft	
	• taking father's role/craft not in Luke, but in the tradition (Mark 6:3)

This sketch of the comparison between John and Jesus functions as most comparisons do: a person of good stature and honor is compared to person of better stature and honor. Each element in the comparison functions to argue for the superiority of Jesus over John; as great as John was ("among those born of women none is greater than John," 7:28), Jesus is greater ("mightier than I . . . whose sandals I am not worthy to untie," 3:16).

We must, however, pay closer attention to the rhetorical comparison of John and Jesus in 3:15–17, where John becomes the **channel** of a less-than-clear **message** to **recipients**, for the **purpose** of answering *their* questioning. The **Sender** seems not to have given *this* **message**; and it matters that John does not initiate this, but only answers a question. The communication flow, then, is askew; John's answer lacks the force of a genuine **channeling**, and his **message** correspondingly is weak. Instead of declaring a name or title for Jesus, John speaks in comparative terms, offering a syncrisis. Of course, it is accurate: Jesus must increase and John decrease (John 3:30).[15] But it stands apart from all previous **messages** about Jesus. What really has John said except that Jesus enjoys a status superior to him? Yes, it is important for a prominent person such as John to speak highly of another person, but this would seem self-evident: "One who is more powerful than I is coming; I am not worthy to untie the thong of his sandals" (3:16). But unlike all others who have ascribed a role and status to Jesus, John labels him with no name, role, or title. In fact, later in Luke's narrative, John remains decidedly uncertain about the role and status of Jesus, so much so that he himself asks the question: "Are you the one who is to come, or are we to wait for another?" (7:20).

The superiority of the "one who is to come" lies in the comparison of their respective baptisms: "I baptize you with water . . . He will baptize you with the Holy Spirit and fire" (3:16). They are compared, also, in terms of other actions. John *imagines* that "every tree therefore that does not bear good fruit is cut down and thrown into the fire"—but throwing trees into the fire will not be John's doing (3:9). Rather he compares his action with that of the coming figure who *performs this deed* himself, but in terms of grain, not trees: "His winnowing-fork is in his hand, to clear his threshing-floor and to gather the wheat into his granary; but the chaff he will burn with unquenchable fire" (3:17). Both figures do virtuous deeds, but those of the coming one are comparatively superior. Thus, the **function** of John's preaching and answering questions is twofold: John offers a baptism of repentance and a cryptic comparison of himself with " he who is coming." The unclarity of John's **message** highlights the superior clarity of that of the ultimate **Sender**, who will immediately make the clearest

---

15. Neyrey and Rohrbaugh, "'He Must Increase, I Must Decrease' (John 3:30)."

possible statement about Jesus's role and status. One might argue that such a moderate **message channeled** by John sets the stage for the **Sender's** own **message** of Jesus's superior status spoken directly to the chief **recipient**, about whom all previous **messages** were directed. It is proper, then, for John's modest **message** to set the stage for God's definitive **message** about Jesus.

Luke 3:21–22

John may not officiate at a ritual for Jesus, but one occurs at the Jordan, and it becomes the most important communication about Jesus thus far in Luke's narrative. After his washing, Jesus "was praying," a very positive commendation of his character. **Where** is Jesus? In the place where washing rituals took place, itself an auspicious place. **When** does communication occur? Was he still in the water? On the riverbank? Nevertheless, the **Sender**, God himself, communicates, not through some **channel**, but by sending his own **message** directly to the **recipient**, about whom all previous **messages** spoke. This fact alone makes the communication of the highest importance and honor, for it was "not done by means of an angel."[16] Jesus, thus ritually purified, becomes the **recipient** of an incomparable **message**. No longer does a mere mortal, even with excellent credentials, **channel** to Jesus a **message** about his role or status; rather, the Author of all honor himself ascribes one to him: "A voice came from heaven, "You are my Son, the Beloved; with you I am well pleased" (3:22). One thing is immediately clear: Jesus now enjoys the very highest status.

The **Sender-of-Senders** establishes this exalted status for Jesus, the **recipient**, in very convincing ways.[17] The tableau begins with the detail that "the heaven was opened"—by the **Sender** of course. Therefore, the heavenly world is directly and immediately impacting the earthly world. The **Sender**, moreover, anoints[18] the head of this **recipient** by causing "the Holy Spirit

16. Goldin, "Not by Means of an Angel."

17. But the **when** and **how** the communication are important parts of the **Sender's message**. The heavens open, allowing for immediate communication between the heavenly and earthly worlds. And, inasmuch as a voice comes down from heaven, it is accompanied by or constitutive of the "anointing" of Jesus: "the Spirit descended upon him in bodily form" (3:22). These are more than stage props, for they are parts of the **message**: The **Sender** of the voice wants it to be appreciated in its importance. See Nolland, *Luke 1—9:20*, 160–61.

18 M. de Jonge, "The Use of the Word 'Anointed' in the Time of Jesus."

to descend upon him in bodily form" (3:22). Thus, like prophets and kings, Jesus is anointed and commissioned. What was formerly ascribed to Jesus is now established. It immediately becomes Jesus's authorization for public voice: "The Spirit of the Lord is upon me, because he has anointed me" (4:18).

Moreover, the dynamics of the theophany themselves imply a role for Jesus. "Spirit," associated with the anointing of prophets and kings for public roles, now serves the same purpose for Jesus. Thus, "anointing" with Spirit implies a public role for Jesus, but one that absorbs that of king and prophet. This specific role was, in fact, the **message** that the **Sender** sent to Mary, the **recipient**: "he will be called the Son of the Most High" (1:32), and "the child to be born will be called holy, the Son of God" (1:35). This "son" will receive "the throne of his father David" (1:32). These earlier declarations must be actualized; Jesus must be established as God's anointed, the premier son. But who may do this? Only the One who has been **sending** previous **messages** about a son! Hence, the voice of God from heaven now speaks directly to Jesus: the **Speaker** (voice from heaven), (no **channel**), speaks a **message** ("my Son"), directly to a **recipient** (Jesus). All previous **messages** are superseded by the **message-of-messages** sent directly by the **Sender-of-Senders**. Jesus is worthy of this status and role, for he is the one "with whom I am well pleased." All previous **messages** about "my Son, the Beloved" are thus resumed here; all roles implied by previous **messages** are now gathered into this role-of-roles, the established Son-of-Sons.

Why does the **Sender** send this **message** to this **recipient**? Several answers are pertinent, which belong to a developing pattern: anointed with God's Spirit, Jesus successfully routs unclean spirits constantly.[19] Finally, God gives him this Spirit to benefit his own disciples: "Being exalted at the right hand of God, and having received from the Father the promise of the Holy Spirit, he has poured out this which you see and hear" (Acts 2:33). In virtue of this, Peter **channels** a **message** from the **Sender-of-Senders** about Jesus to special **recipients**: This **message** explicitly declares the establishment of the ultimate role of Jesus: "Let the whole house of Israel know that God has made him both Lord and Christ" (Acts 2:36).

Therefore, before Jesus begins speaking in public, Luke has elaborately established his ethos from birth to adulthood, by means of intensifying **messages** about his status and role, which are **channeled** by figures of solid credentials. In terms of communication theory, then, the **Sender-of-Senders**

---

19. Essential here is DeMaris, "The Baptism of Jesus."

constantly speaks throughout Luke 1–3 about Jesus. At first, God employs **channels** of recognized social status, who **channel** a remarkable **message**, i.e., about the roles and statuses of Jesus, for the **purpose** of establishing his worthiness to speak. When Luke 1–4 is considered as a whole, the communication about the ethos of Jesus reaches its climax in 3:21–22, whereby Jesus, now an adult, is authorized by the **Sender** to exercise public voice.

The Sender-of-Senders: The Primary Storyteller in Luke 1–4

Concentration on the communication model for reading Luke 1–4 yields an immediate and significant result. Although all the **messages** are about Jesus, their **Sender** must be given paramount attention. The **Sender** is none other than the God of Israel. The magnitude of this observation requires us to reexamine our perspective on Luke's beginning chapters, because it urges us to consider "the neglected factor in New Testament theology," namely, God.[20] It has been quipped that modern readers of the Gospels are "christo-monists"; we focus completely or mostly on Jesus, with consideration of God as a minor or second-order character. That is, the **message**, i.e., "Jesus," fills the screen; yet the **Sender**, whose plan and purpose continually drive the narrative, is rarely allowed to appear on commentators' monitors. Yet the **Sender's** active role in Luke 1–4 is to **send** continuously various **messages**, which, like eggs, take time to hatch. The **messages**, moreover, always vary in content, because the **Sender** remains constantly in charge of the narrative.

Consideration of God has not been totally wanting. Various articles and monographs on God in Luke–Acts have been published;[21] but only occasionally do they include mention of God in an index of subjects.[22]

In a seminal article on the beginning of Luke, Joel Green argues that "Luke 1:5—2:52 initiates a narrative above all centered on God whose aim it is to bring salvation in all its fulness to all. However, the story of Jesus' birth and childhood do not really *introduce* this God or this aim, nor does

---

20. Dahl, "The Neglected Factor in New Testament Theology."
21. Squires, *The Plan of God in Luke–Acts*; York, *The Last Shall Be First*.
22. Even here, interest rests on "God" under certain aspects, such as "Father" and "salvation history" (Fitzmyer, *The Gospel according to Luke*, 179–87); the will or plan of God (Cosgrove, "The Divine DEI in Luke–Acts"; Mowrey, "The Divine Hand and the Divine Plan in the Lukan Passion"; and "prophecy-fulfilment"). Because scholarly attention is mainly focused on the **message**, the dominant role of the **Sender** is diminished.

it pretend to do so."[23] He argues further that the individual stories of Jesus, Peter, and others

> are related within larger narrative sequences whose interest transcends their individual deeds. Luke is concerned with how these events, those narrated in the Gospel and in Acts, are understood as divine events . . . [T]hese events are incomplete in themselves, and must be understood in relation to a wider interpretative framework . . . In 1:5—2:52 he will "begin" his narrative with the events surrounding the births of John and Jesus, but for him this is not really the beginning. They relate to something else, something prior. As 1:5—2:52 make clear, they relate to God's purpose, evident in the Old Testament and the history of God's people, as its culmination.[24]

As Green sees it, "the function of Luke 1:5—2:52 is a harbinger of the story to come."[25] The only actor constantly onstage is God, the protagonist and the **Sender** of many messages.

Green's understanding of beginnings is quite compatible with discussions of them found in Aristotle and Cicero, whose ideas will be discussed in a subsequent chapter on "how 'beginnings' begin." And he is accurate when he states, "As Luke's employment of Israel's Scriptures in Luke 1:5—2:52 demonstrates, the proper 'beginning' for his narrative is *there*, in the past, in God's redemptive purpose as set forth in the Scriptures. Luke is not introducing a *new* story, but continuing an old one."[26] The narrative, as he describes it, concludes with this summary: "The God who has been working redemptively *still is*, now, and especially, in Jesus. This reality is clarified magnificently in the narrative of Jesus' birth and childhood."[27]

Green's argument can be sharpened by reference to the study by Nils Dahl on Abraham in Luke–Acts. Dahl works out of the framework of prophecy-fulfilment, and chooses to focus on the earliest un-ambiguous reference to God's promise, which is to Abraham. As he argues, God's word/promise to Abraham is the beginning of Israel's history.[28] This is clearly

---

23. Green, "The Problem of a Beginning," 63 (italics original).
24. Green, "The Problem of a Beginning," 63.
25. Green, "The Problem of a Beginning," 61.
26. Green, "The Problem of a Beginning," 61 (italics original).
27. Green, "The Problem of a Beginning," 67 (italics original).
28. Dahl, *Jesus in the Memory of the Early Church*, 72–73.

argued by Stephen in Acts 7:2–8, 17, 32 and then by Paul in Acts 13:32–33.[29] Then, Dahl links these references to Luke 1, where we find two clear references to God's promise/covenant to Abraham, first in Mary's praise (1:54–55) and in that of Zechariah (1:72–73).[30] Thus, Dahl describes Luke's "theology of history," which puts front and center the active role of God, in regard to God's promise to Abraham, its realization in the time of Jesus, and its continuation as Abraham is declared the father of many nations. God's promise begins, then is partially realized, and finally extends into the time of the early church. In terms of the communication model, God is the continuous **Sender** of a **message**, which is about Jesus and much more.

Green's study, reinforced by that of Dahl, persuades us that our use of the communication model serves a significant purpose in understanding Luke because it makes us attend to the primary storyteller in the narrative, namely, the single **Sender** who speaks through many **channels**. Of course, one may put emphasis on the **messages**, but they are remarks awaiting realization; in Luke 1–2, they are important statements, but ones which need to be established. But how inadequate it is to ignore or downplay the continuous actions of the **Sender**! The repeated actions of the **Sender**, which communicate that the various **messages** are of course completely under the **Sender's** guidance, drive the narrative. In this case, therefore, the role of the **Sender** alone gives the **messages** their importance. Finally, until the **Sender/Speaker** speaks directly to the **recipient** (3:21–22), the **messages** are mere plans by the **Sender/Speaker**, awaiting establishment by the remarkable phenomenon of the **Sender/Speaker** speaking directly to the **recipient** Jesus, and by the **message** spoken setting Jesus's role in motion. Therefore, using the communication model, we may discern certain rhetorical strategies often left obscure or misinterpreted. The dominant actor in Luke 1–4 is the **Sender**, who is the God of Israel, the master storyteller, who speaks constantly about Jesus, not to him.

Aristotle, Rhetoric, and Communication

Aristotle was aware of the distinct roles of speaker and listener, and of the materials needed to make a successful communication. To be sure, he did not know the communication model described above, nor the modern jargon used to label its various elements. Nevertheless, in various places in his

29. Dahl, *Jesus in the Memory of the Early Church*, 73, 78–79.
30. Dahl, *Jesus in the Memory of the Early Church*, 80–81.

Rhetorica, Aristotle spoke of materials needed for successful communication as parts of proper orations—elements which directly correlate with the elements in the communication model. We are hardly attempting a complete overview of his *Rhetorica*, but only identification of the items that correspond to the elements of the communication model we have studied.

> **(Re: exordium)** "Every speech is composed of three parts: the speaker, the subject of which he treats, and the person to whom it is addressed" (1.2.3.); "(forms of exordia) ... They are derived from the speaker, the hearer, the subject, and the opponent." (3.14.7).

1. Who Speaks? (Sender)

A successful speaker should possess these qualities: "the speaker should show himself to be of a certain character and should know how to put the judge into a certain frame of mind."[31] Further, "the speaker should show himself to be possessed of certain qualities and that his hearers should think that he is disposed in a certain way toward them ... For the orator to produce conviction three qualities are necessary: good sense [*pronēsis*], virtue [*aretē*], and goodwill [*eunoia*]" (2.1.2–5).

Second, to be successful, a speaker must satisfy certain social expectations, which have to do with external and internal goods. "External goods include noble birth, numerous friends, wealth, numerous and good children ... bodily excellences such as health, beauty, strength ... a good reputation, honor and virtue ... Internal goods are those of mind and body; external goods are noble birth, friends, wealth, and honor" (1.5.4).[32]

Third, besides being well-informed about a topic (*phronēsis*), a successful speaker must be known for honorable achievements: "Since praise is founded on actions, and acting according to moral purpose is characteristic of the worthy man, we must endeavor to show that a man is acting in that manner ... Praise is language that sets forth greatness of virtue; hence it is necessary to show that a man's actions are virtuous ... Achievements, in fact, are signs of moral habit" (1.9.32–34).

---

31. The "character" is "trustworthiness" (see also 1.2.3–6; 3.16.8–9).

32. Although Aristotle does not formally define an encomium, he knows it traditional components. This fact will prove very useful when we consider the formal genre encomium as part of the progymnasmata. Aristotle identifies three regular topics of an encomium: A noble birth and education ... achievements/virtues" (*Rhet.* 1.9.33–34).

2. What Is Spoken? (Message)

In the most general terms, Aristotle distinguishes three types of rhetoric, each one of which has its own purpose or message. "We must distinguish between each of them individually, that is, what the three kinds of Rhetoric, deliberative, epideictic, and forensic, are concerned with" (1.3.9).

— deliberative: ". . . the most important subjects, about which all men deliberate and orators harangue, are five in number: ways and means, war and peace, defense of the country, imports and exports, legislation" (1.4.7).

— epideictic: "Since praise is founded on action, and acting according to moral purpose is characteristic of the worthy man, we must endeavor to show that a man is acting in that manner, and it is useful that it should appear that he has done so on several occasions" (1.9.32).

— forensic: "[concerning accusation and defense] Three things have to be considered; first, the nature and number of the motives which lead men to act unjustly; secondly, what is the state of mind of those who so act; thirdly, the character and dispositions of those who are exposed to injustice" (1.10.1).

Therefore, the rhetorical message corresponds to the purpose of the speech.

Expanding on this, Cicero comments on what an orator should say, after praising Aristotle for the development of specific "topics." What to say, states Cicero, depends on "a system developed by Aristotle for inventing arguments so that we may come upon them by a rational system without wandering about" (Cicero, *Top.* 1.2); and "this is the end of the rules for the invention of arguments, so that if you have journeyed through definition, partition, etymology, conjugates, genus, species, similarity, differences, contraries, adjuncts, consequents, antecedents, contradictions, causes, effects, and comparison of things greater, less and equal, no region of arguments remains to be explored" (Cicero, *Top.* 18.71).

3. To Whom Is the Speech Spoken? (Recipients)

Aristotle acknowledges different types of hearers, who must be addressed appropriately. "The kinds of Rhetoric are three in number, corresponding to *three kinds of hearers*. For every speech is composed of three parts: the speaker, the subject of which he treats, and the person to whom it is addressed, I mean the hearers, to whom the end or object of the speech refers. Now the hearer must necessarily be either a mere spectator or a judge." (*Rhet.* 1.3.1 [italics added]).

A successful speaker, moreover, must know what emotions he wishes to arouse in his hearers. In regard to this, Aristotle spends considerable time defining and displaying a wide variety of emotions that can be aroused and appealed to, thus accommodating a hearer (*Rhet.* 2.1.8—2.11.7). Hence, it is not just a matter of **what** a speaker says but also a consideration of **how** a hearer would hear: "The object of an appeal to the hearer is to make him well-disposed or to arouse his indignation, and sometime to engage his attention or the opposite . . . Hearers pay most attention to things that are important, that concern their own interests, that are astonishing, that are agreeable" (3.14.7).

Hearers (i.e., **recipients**) hear differently according to their developmental age, and so Aristotle urges that they be addressed differently: "Let us now describe the nature of the characters of men [i.e., audience] according to their emotions, habits, age, and fortunes":

— "The **young**, as to character, are ready to desire and carry out what they desire . . . Changeable in their desires and soon tiring of them, they desire with extreme ardor, but soon cool" (2.12.3).

— "**Older men and those who have passed their prime** have in most cases characters opposite to those of the young . . . They are positive about nothing, and in everything show an excessive lack of energy. They always 'think,' but 'know' nothing . . . They are malicious . . . looking upon the worst side of everything" (2.13.1–3).

— "It is evident that the character of those **in the prime of life** will be the mean between that of the other two. At this age, men are neither overconfident, which would show rashness, nor too fearful, but preserving a right attitude in regard to both, neither trusting nor distrusting all, but judging in accordance with actual facts" (2.14.1–2).

Aristotle returns to this topic later in his *Rhetorica*, attending then to the issue of style, that is, what is appropriate for a given character (and audience).[33]

---

33. "Character also may be expressed by the proof from signs, because to each class and habit there is an appropriate style. I mean class in reference to age—child, man, or old man; to sex—man or woman; to country—Lacedaemonian or Thessalian" (*Rhet.*

4. Why Does a Speaker Speak? (Purpose) "Inasmuch as there are three types of rhetoric, the purpose of each differs, but each has a distinctive purpose, depending on the type of rhetoric" (1.3.5).

- "The end of the deliberative speaker is the expedient and the harmful."
- "The end of the forensic speaker is the just and the unjust."
- "The end of those who praise and blame is the honorable and the disgraceful" (1.3.5).

In general, the aim of rhetoric is persuasion: "Rhetoric then may be defined as the faculty of discovering the possible means of persuasion in reference to any subject whatever" (1.2.1).[34]

In composing his *Rhetorica*, Aristotle describes a process of communication that had the same elements as a modern model of communication. Aristotle, however, was instructing orators how they *should* speak, whereas those who use modern communication modeling analyze what has *already* been written or spoken. But both consider the same categories: the **sender/ speaker**, who sends an appropriate **message** to specific but diverse **hearers/ recipients**, by appropriate **means** (in spoken word, in prose writing—always with concern for style and rhetorical skills), for a **purpose**.

Classicists, Rhetoric, and Communication

The communication model has been appropriated also by some classicists. Jakob Wisse studied the rhetorical elements of a proper exordium, namely, ethos and pathos, according to modern communication theory. In his monograph, he traced the history of these two items from Aristotle to Roman times. But simply to repeat the words of the ancients would not serve his purpose, so he chose to express his discussion of them in terms of "a

---

3.3.7.6–7).

34. Aristotle is also concerned with how a speech or argument is constructed according to rhetorical aims. For example, "proof of an argument" depends on the 'logos' of his speech, which he must craft in proper rhetorical form: "Now the proofs furnished by the speech are of three kinds. The first depends on the moral character of the speaker, the second upon putting the hearer into a certain frame of mind, the third upon the speech (*logos*) itself" (1.2.3). Furthermore, an adequate speech has certain parts that are necessary to make a proper argument: "So the necessary parts of a speech are the statement of the case and proof. These divisions are appropriate to every speech, and at the most the parts are four in number: exordium, statement, proof, epilogue" (3.1.3.4).

simple model of communication."[35] He presents in this figure the essential components of the model he follows:

speaker		audience
	speech	
	(message)	
(sender)		(receiver)

Wisse applies this to Aristotle's definition of a "rational argument," that is, how an argument is made: "Now the proofs furnished by the speech are of three kinds. The first depends on the moral character [*ethos*] of the speaker, the second upon putting the hearer into a certain frame of mind [*pathos*], the third upon the speech itself [*logos*]" (*Rhet.* 1.2.3). Wisse observes "a simple connection between rational argument (*logos*), *ethos* and *pathos* on the one hand, and the corresponding entities of the (communication) model on the other":

arguments seem bound up with the message (*logos*),

ethos seems to be bound up with the sender,

and *pathos* intends an effect of the message on the receiver.

Thus, he concludes, "All three entities play their part, the sender as well as the message and the receiver"[36]:

(1) starting from the **sender**: the speaker is presented as likeable, etc.;

(2) starting from the **message**: form or content or tone of the speech suggests that the speaker is trustworthy in the eyes of an audience;

(3) starting from the **receiver**: the audience is made to regard the speaker as likeable, etc.

Wisse's use of a communication model serves one important purpose, namely, that although ancient rhetoricians employed their own terminology,

---

35. Wisse, *Ethos and Pathos from Aristotle to Cicero*. He builds on continental studies, such as Bühler, *Sprachtheorie*, with further mention of researchers such as Roman Jakobson

36 Wisse, *Ethos and Pathos from Aristotle to Cicero*, 7.

their discourse corresponds to modern communication models and so validates reading Luke 1–4 in the same way.

Summary and Conclusions

A particular selection of Luke's narrative has been excerpted for careful study: episodes in 1:5—3:22 in which some authorized person speaks a message to someone else about Jesus. These messages occur in conversations, which often include responses to what was told, often intensifying the message of the communication. Only direct statements were examined, that is, messages spoken by narrative characters, not comments by Luke. We chose to examine them in terms of a common model of communication to make explicit who was saying what to whom, by means of what channel and for what purpose. There necessarily was much repetition, but since Luke himself decided on this, the extent of our task was warranted. What, then, do we know when we read Luke 1–4 in this way?

1. God, of course, is the ultimate **Sender** of all communication—the **Sender-of-Senders**. Inasmuch as God's word is always of paramount importance, the consistent recognition of **God-as-Sender** elevates all of the communications to the highest level. When God speaks, all (should) listen.

2. It was a biblical axiom that Israel needed a **channel** such as Moses to mediate God's word to them. When Israel stood before Sinai, the people pleaded with Moses, "You speak to us, and we will listen; but do not let God speak to us, *or we will die*" (Exod 20:18–19).[37] Whether they are individual persons such as Moses, or brokers or mediators or angels or prophets, God's word was traditionally communicated through a **channel** or **mediator**. And this likewise happens when Luke narrates that God **sends** a **message** by means of appropriate **channels**, either angel or prophet.

3. The **Sender's message** is always about Jesus, indicating the role or status God ascribes to him. Yet the content of the **messages** varies, because the **Sender** gathers together many previous **messages** spoken in Israel's history. Nevertheless, the communication constantly ascribes to Jesus exceptionally high roles and statuses.

37. The midrashic elaborations of this are numerous and cogent; see Neyrey, "I Said: 'You are Gods.'"

4. The **purpose** of the communication seems evident. God, who is the ultimate ascriber of honor and status, gradually establishes the ethos of Jesus so that when a mature elder, he should enjoy authority appropriate for public voice. The roles for Jesus contained in the various **messages** are all public ones, which together authorize him for public voice.

5. The repetitiousness of the communication establishes its importance by the very fact of its repetition, namely, that the **Sender**, God, constantly has something important to say about Jesus.

6. The correlation of the modern communication model and Aristotle's *Rhetorica* serves two purposes: first, it confirms the validity of using a modern model to read an ancient text, and, second, it indicates the antiquity of thinking in these terms. The correlation, moreover, argues that its use is not an unwarranted imposition of an inappropriate model on an ancient document.

7. Wisse's reading of Aristotle's *Rhetorica* in terms of the communication model also argues that those trained in the classics are likewise reading Aristotle correctly when they read with modern lenses.

8. Would a modern reader come to this without the use of a communication model? Possibly, if they were acquainted with rhetoric. But knowledge of the rhetoric of communication gives security to readers' perceptions. A modern reader is hearing Luke as did his original audience.

CHAPTER 2

Jesus in Social-Science Perspective

WE CONTINUE TO USE social-science models for reading Luke's narrative, employing two of great importance for those who would read a first-century document on its own cultural terms. First, anthropological research has shown that modern persons differ from people of many other cultures in the way the human person is understood. In the world of Luke and Jesus, persons regularly understood themselves as embedded in others, in particular, in family, clan, and ethnos. They are regularly introduced in kinship terms, as "son of so-and-so": In his Gospel, Luke identifies "John, son of Zechariah" (3:2); "James, son of Alphaeus" (6:15–16); "Zechariah, of the division of Abijah" and "his wife, of the daughters of Aaron" (1:5); and "Joseph of the house of David" (1:27). In Acts the bystanders hearing the apostles on Pentecost comment, "Are not these who are speaking Galileans? How is it that we hear them in our own native language? Parthians, Medes, Elamites, and residents of Mesopotamia, Judea and Cappadocia?" (2:7–9).[1] Second, cultural research has also shown that the premier value of people in the ancient world was "honor," that is, the worth or respect one has in the eyes of others. So, as we seek to know how Luke created an ethos for Jesus to have public voice, we need to examine what this would look like according

---

1. These identification markers locate a person in his social context, not as individuals. Aristotle argues that children would have the same distinctions as their parents (*Rhet.* 1.5.50). It was a common cultural expectation that children would be chips off the old block (see Deut 23:2; 2 Kgs 9:22; Isa 57:3; Sir 23:25–26; 30:7). We are told, like father, like son (Matt 11:27) and like mother, like daughter (Ezek 16:44). Besides the Scriptures, Plato stated it clearly: "They were good because they sprang from good fathers" (*Menex.* 237); likewise, Quintilian: "Persons are generally regarded as having some resemblance to their parents and ancestors, a resemblance which leads to their living disgracefully or honorably, as the case may be" (*Inst. Orat.* 5.10.24).

to the cultural canons of his time. Without them, Jesus will unfortunately be like us in all things, a case of ethnocentrism run amuck.

Group-Oriented Persons

All people may be one hundred percent human, but not all live that humanity in the same way. How difficult it is for modern Euro-Americans to understand that not everyone in the world is independent and free to pursue his or her dreams, marriage partners, ambitions, and careers. Not everyone has a First Amendment in a Constitution that protects freedom of speech; not all have a Hyde Park where anyone may say what they please atop a soapbox. In fact, we individualists are confused or put off by those of other cultures whose success depends on accepting the role and status that is assigned them.[2] In those different cultures, group-oriented persons are known socially, not psychologically. To know a person, one has to know (1) a person's clan and family; (2) an individual's place of origin, village or city,[3] (3) a person's inherited craft or trade,[4] (4) the group or party to which a person belongs,[5] and (5) the social expectations of the groups within which a person is embedded. In short, individuals are known in terms of cultural stereotypes,[6] including gender.[7] To know one of them, one must know their ascribed role and status, something that they do not choose for themselves. Israelites were wont to say that all is due to God's "plan and purpose," which extends to every individual person. Writing to the Corinthians, Paul assumed that God, has "arranged the organs in the body, each one of them, as God chooses" (1 Cor 12:18). Paul also wrote, "There is no authority except from God, and those authorities that exist have been instituted by God" (Rom 13:1). Thus, a virtuous group-oriented person is exhorted, "Let each

---

2. This discussion is not new to New Testament scholarship; see Malina and Neyrey, *Portraits of Paul*, 1–18 and especially 153–201.

3. "Jesus of Nazareth" (4:34; 18:37); "Joseph, from the Judean town of Arimathea" (23:50).

4. "Fishermen" (5:1–11); "steward of Herod" (8:3); "estate steward" (16:1); and "tenant farmer" (20:10).

5. "There were Pharisees and teachers of the law sitting by . . ." (5:17); "There came to him Sadducees, who say that there is no resurrection . . ." (20:27).

6. On the conventionality of thinking in terms of stereotypes in the ancient world, see Malina and Neyrey, *Portraits of Paul*, 117–20, 150–51, and 169–74.

7. For convenience's sake, see Neyrey, "Jesus, Gender and the Gospel of Matthew."

of you lead the life that the Lord has assigned, to which God called you." (1 Cor 7:17). This is hardly the great American Dream.

Hence, we should strive to understand Jesus and Luke in their own cultural context, not ours. This means that, in stark contrast to us, Jesus (and Luke) was anything but an individualist.[8] Cultural anthropologists would label him a dyadic person,[9] a group-oriented person. Thus, Jesus learned the social code of depending on others to tell him who he was and what was expected of him—a social identity and social expectations reinforced by responses conferring on him honor or shame. For example, as a boy Jesus claims that he is following his Father's will by remaining in Jerusalem after his parents had left ("Did you not know that I must be in my Father's house?" [2:47]), nevertheless he goes down to Nazareth and is "obedient to them" (2:51), accepting their authority as paramount. It was the only respectable thing for a boy to do. How often does Jesus state that he acts in "obedience" only to God? It is God, and God alone, who ascribes to him his role and status: understanding this as Luke's argument is the aim of reading Luke 1–4 in terms of the communications model. From Luke's first remarks about Jesus, it is narrated that Jesus is a typical group-oriented person. We saw in the last chapter that God and many agents speaking for God ascribe to Jesus his role and status—that is, his public identity.

Therefore, to know Jesus, one must know his family and kin. Luke tells us these data repeatedly, whether through an angelic **channel** (1:31–33, 35) or by God, the **Sender/Speaker** (3:21–22). Luke himself declares Jesus's generational and geographical origins: Jesus belongs to the house of David (2:4), and Luke's genealogy establishes Jesus's kin and ancestors as honorable (3:23–38). As regards Jesus's geographical origins, Luke narrates that he is born in David's royal city (2:4, 11). Circumcision, moreover, establishes him as a member of the house of Israel. Jesus associates with men who are fishermen, like their fathers: "James and John, sons of Zebedee, who were partners of Simon" (5:10). He himself inherits his father's craft as a worker in wood.[10] He belonged to no group, such as the Pharisees.

---

8. Social-science scholars have long researched dyadic or group-oriented persons; for immediate access to the conversation, see Triandis, "Cross-Cultural Studies in Individualism and Collectivism"; and Schwartz, "Individualism-Collectivism."

9. Important studies that use the cultural studies just noted depend largely on the scholarship of Bruce J. Malina, including Malina, "Dealing with Biblical (Mediterranean) Characters"; Malina and Neyrey, "First-Century Personality"; and Malina and Neyrey, *Portraits of Paul*, 1–63, 225–31.

10. In social-science terminology, Jesus's "nurture and training" came by way of a process called "socialization." See Neyrey, "'How Does This Man Have Learning.'"

Although he became disembedded from his family, Jesus immediately became re-embedded in a new Father, whom he honors above all things, and whose will he knows and follows. And so, all the names and titles ascribed to Jesus from Luke 1:26 to Luke 5:30 have been validly made by God, **Sender/Speaker** and by God's **messengers/channels**. Jesus never claims any role or status for himself; indeed, no group-oriented person should. All of his credentials are given him by prominent people who authorize him to have public voice. His ethos, then, is a social construction.

Excursus: Comparative Table of Salient Features of Modern and Ancient Persons

This table is the appendix to a volume dedicated to describing Paul as a group-oriented person.[11] The categories chosen for comparison here represent those emphasized in the cultural studies upon which the book is based.

Modern Euro-American Individualism	Ancient Group-Orientation
Basic Psychology of Individualistic Person:	Basic Psychology of Group-Oriented Person:
Individualists are socialized to think of self as individuals and to relate to others as individuals.	Group-oriented persons are socialized to think of themselves as group members and to relate to others stereotypically.
They think psychologically and individualistically and avoid stereotypes; they represent themselves and their opinions alone.	They think "socially," in group terms, and employ inherited stereotypes.
They are unpredictable and always changing.	Individuals and groups are quite predictable and unchanging.
Singly and corporately they are responsible for social choices: marriage, economy, political decisions.	God (fate, fortune, providence) alone ordains all social arrangements and outcomes.
Mobility and Change: Individualistic persons are expected to experience a great deal of geographical and social mobility and status change.	**Mobility and Change:** Group-oriented persons are expected to experience little if any geographical and social mobility or status change over many generations.

---

11. Malina and Neyrey, *Portraits of Paul*, 226–31.

Basic Beliefs: The individual is believed to be the primary reality, with society a second-order, artificial or derived construct.	**Basic Beliefs:** Society (group) is believed to be the primary reality, while the individual is a second-order, artificial or derived construct.
Salient Features: An individualist prizes self-reliance, individual happiness and success, self-realization, psychological gratification.	**Salient Features:** Group-oriented persons favor group well-being, prudence (being controlled by in-group advice), justice (performing group obligations), temperance (a sense of shame, concern for status), courage (endurance, strength of character).
Kinship: Because kinship relations are independent of individual choice and will, they can be dismissed to a considerable extent.	**Kinship:** Because kinship relations are independent of individual choice and will, they are perceived as God-given, sacred.
Religion: Religion is a freestanding institution, concerned with the moral order. Religion is an individual concern operating through voluntary association.	**Religion:** Religion, embedded in kinship and/or politics, is concerned with the moral order. Political religion is a public concern, controlled by elites and operating to maintain the status quo that is public order. Domestic religion is a kinship concern, controlled by the head of the family and operating to maintain family integrity.
Success: Success is the outcome of free competition among individuals in an open market.	**Success:** Success consists in living up to and maintaining one's inherited social status.
Meaning of Life: The ultimate meaning of life stands quite apart from conforming to the purely procedural and institutionally variable rules and regulations that surround the individual in society; self-integration is what counts.	**Meaning of Life:** The ultimate meaning of life consists precisely in conforming to the purely procedural and institutionally variable rules and regulations that surround the individual in society; social integration is what counts.

Which kind of person best describes Jesus in the Gospel of Luke? And so, what would his ethos correspondingly be? Jesus is portrayed as a group-oriented person, whose profile is sketched in the right column. Jesus's ethos is a tissue of stereotypes: he is a member of the house of Israel, people gathered by God's covenant (1:32–33). He thinks socially, in terms of stereotypes ("Chorazin! Bethsaida!" 10:13); he speaks proverbs and maxims (4:23). Jesus relates to groups of peers in the local synagogue (4:16–29), who are often men of the same trade; and he interacts with groups such as the Pharisees, scribes, lawyers (11:42–52), and Sadducees (20:27–40).

Ideally, Jesus should never have left Nazareth or assumed the role of teacher, except for the fact that he was sent to do so (4:43). If true to form, Jesus's behavior should have been quite predictable (obeying the higher authority; keeping the law, especially the Sabbath; staying where he belonged), except for the fact that God sent him to do otherwise. Jesus takes all of his identity from others (1:31–35; 2:11, 30–32; 3:21–22; 9:18–20). Knowing what his group expects of him, he should be living up to those expectations, not acting like a maverick (8:19–21). Kinship relations are paramount, even if he leaves them to become ultimately embedded in another Father (4:1–12), with another mother and brothers (8:21). Success for Jesus means total faithfulness to God and complete acceptance of the role and status ascribed him by God. The meaning of life for him consists in conformity to rules given by two fathers (2:49, 51). Therefore, the ethos that Luke constructs for Jesus would necessarily be a group-oriented one, something both Luke and his audience would recognize and honor. The ethos of Jesus may take thirty or so years to complete, but that is Luke's task in the early chapters of his narrative.

Honor-and-Shame Orientation

We take it as proven that the cultural world of Jesus pivoted around the premiere value of honor (and shame).[12] Inasmuch as the identity, role, and status of individual persons were ascribed to them, as noted above, there correspondingly existed a value system whereby all ascribed remarks about a person as well as the choreography of acquiring and maintaining this value was a culturally shared given. If success for a group-oriented person lay in conforming to the rules prescribed by others, then honor is the award for keeping them. Group-oriented personality and honor, then, are two sides of the same coin.

"Honor" means *social value*, worth, respect, and importance[13] as others see it. In a group-oriented world, most honor was ascribed by parents,

---

12. The cultural understanding of honor has been established by many scholars, such as Bordieu, "The Sentiment of Honour in Kabyle Society"; and Gilmore, ed., *Honor and Shame*; and Peristiany and Pitt-Rivers, eds., *Honor and Grace in Anthropology*.

13. New Testament scholars have shown impressively the importance of honor in the Gospels and the letters of Paul; see Malina, *The New Testament World* (3rd ed.), 27–57; Malina and Neyrey, "Honor and Shame in Luke–Acts"; Moxnes, "Honor and Shame";

kin, tribe, and so forth, and approved by neighbors, synagogue, and village. How important, then, is the reaction of the crowds, which award and confirm Jesus's standing: "A report concerning him went out through all the surrounding country. He taught in their synagogues, being glorified by all" (4:14–15; see 4:37; 5:15, 25–26; 7:17; 8:39). Honor claims made on behalf of an individual must be accepted by others; otherwise they are but "vainglory." Thus, in terms of the gender stereotype, a son has more honor than a daughter, a firstborn son more than his siblings, and the son of a large landowner more than the son of a subsistent peasant working his or another's land. Because of the singular importance of the value of honor (and shame), we offer the following excursus.

Excursus: Honor and Shame

1. Sources: (a) ascribed, by birth[14] or authorization; (b) achieved, by competition in the arenas of politics or the military,[15] or by athletic and aesthetic achievements.[16]

2. Essence: social worth or standing that a group claims for an individual, which must be acknowledged by others.[17]

3. Symbolism: (a) indicated by one's name (generational and geographical),[18] (b) discernible in one's ascribed role and status, (c)

---

and Neyrey, *Honor and Shame in the Gospel of Matthew*.

14. See Rohrbaugh, "Luke's Jesus," 31–37.

15. Honor, of course, was earned by the diminutive David killing the giant Goliath. The Maccabean heroes gained great honor either by defeating their foes or by dying nobly at their hands.

16. "How honored Alcibiades was when his chariots won three of the top four prizes in a championship race (Thucydides 6.16.2–3), a victory so famous that it was remembered and celebrated for centuries" (Plutarch *Alcibiades* 11.1–2; cf. Plutarch, *Table-Talk* 674D–75D).

17. Josephus celebrates the Hasmoneans because of both ascribed and achieved honor: "Theirs was a splendid and renowned house because of both their lineage and their priestly office, as well as the things which its founders achieved on behalf of the nation" (*Ant.* 14.490).

18. "Some [names] are given for some special reasons, such as the titles of Wise, Great, Pius" (Quintilian, *Inst. Orat.* 5.10.30); other names express role and status, such as "Caesar," "King," "Pharaoh," and "Consul."

expressed in public awards,[19] (d) displayed by various forms of conspicuous consumption,[20] and (e) manifested by actions of courage, power, and prowess.

4. Rhetorical forms expressive of it: both ceremonies and commissioning rituals, as well as chreia and challenge/riposte exchanges.

5. Cultural importance: paramount value that distinguishes one city from all others,[21] and mortals from animals;[22] lack or loss of honor means social death.

In the cultural world of the Bible, God alone ascribes paramount honor, who might use mediators or channels to declare it in specific circumstances: "Let all the house of Israel know assuredly that God has made him Lord and Christ" (Acts 2:33, 36). Other such persons who ascribe honor include the Roman Caesar, who could appoint a procurator, such as Pontius Pilate. Even the Herods had whatever honorable status they enjoyed because of the pleasure of whichever Caesar gave it to them.

---

19. Aristotle narrates what honor actually looked like: "The constituents of honor are: sacrifices; commemoration, in verse or prose; privileges; grants of land; front seats at civic celebrations; state burial; statues; public maintenance; among foreigners, obeisance and giving place; and such presents as are among various bodies of men regarded as marks of honor. For a present is not only a bestowal of a piece of property, but also a token of honor" (*Rhet.* 1.5.9).

20. Besides the clothing they wore, elites claimed honor through the display of their table setting and the manner in which they dined: "With no one to look on, wealth becomes sightless indeed and bereft of radiance. For when the rich man dines with his wife or intimates, he lets his tables of citrus-wood and golden beakers rest in peace and uses common furnishings, and his wife attends it without her gold and purple and dressed in plain attire. But when a banquet—that is, a spectacle and a show—is got up and the drama of wealth brought on, 'out of the ships he fetches the urns and tripods' (*Il.* 23.259), the repositories of the lamps are given no rest, the cups are changed, the cup-bearers are made to put on new attire, nothing is left undisturbed, gold, silver, or jeweled plate, the owners thus confessing that their wealth is for others" (Plutarch, *On Love of Wealth* 528B; see Plutarch, *Table-Talk* 679B).

21. "Athenians excel all others not so much in singing or in stature or in strength, as in love of honor (*philotimia*), which is the strongest incentive to deeds of honor and renown" (Xenophon, *Mem.* 3.3.13).

22. "In this man differs from other animals—I mean, in this craving for honor. In meat and drink and sleep and sex all creatures alike seem to take pleasure; but love of honor (*philotimia*) is rooted neither in the brute beasts nor in every human being. But they in whom is implanted a passion for honor and praise, these are they who differ most from beasts of the field, these are accounted men and not mere human beings (Xenophon, *Hiero* 7.3).

Later in this book we will consider the progymnastic genre chreia, which dramatizes a particular way of maintaining honor. Because so many of Jesus's public actions are challenged by others, it is important to know that they are narrated in a typical genre to display both Jesus's reputation for prowess and his honorable defense of it.

When viewing Luke 1–4 in terms of the cultural value of honor, we observe that all of Jesus's honor is ascribed to him, and not achieved. God, the most honorable figure in the cosmos, ascribes him the highest roles and status, which are necessarily the most honorable.

What honor does God ascribe to Jesus?

- "He will be great, and will be called the son of the Most High" (1:32)
- "The child . . . will be holy, the son of God" (1:35)
- "To you is born a Savior, who is Christ the Lord" (2:11)
- "You are my Son, the Beloved, with whom I am well pleased" (3:22)
- "This Jesus God raised up . . . exalted at the right hand of God . . . God has made him both Lord and Christ." (Acts 2:32–36)

God, then, has the first and last word about the honor of Jesus.

Therefore, when Luke establishes an ethos for Jesus, he necessarily builds it according to the understandings of honor in his culture. An honorable ethos for Jesus is his narrative task. And the honor that he perceives Jesus as deserving he necessarily builds according to the cultural conventions of his time. Moreover, honor ascribed must be acknowledged by some public. We noted above how quickly a favorable "report" spread abroad, which acknowledged the role and status which Jesus claimed in various synagogues. This was sufficient to attract critics and challengers. Thus, in terms of the paramount value of Luke's cultural world, the ethos of Jesus is established; and so, Jesus should be considered worthy to have public voice."

Summary and Conclusions

When reading literature from a culture different from one's own, special care must be taken to avoid ethnocentrism. No, they are not "just like us." As the melody goes, "Two different worlds, we live in two different worlds." The two social-science models presented in this chapter are proposed as necessary ways to understand ancient texts such as Luke's narrative, because each provides a modern reader with culturally specific ways of entering the world of the ancient author and his narrative. This is particularly true when we try to appreciate what kind of person Jesus was (as Luke portrayed him). We will learn more about Luke himself in the last chapter of this book when we study the prologue to his Gospel. But in the narrative from 1:5 through 4:30, we are privy to the ways Luke created for Jesus an ethos appropriate for his culture. For Jesus to be recognizable, Luke had to present him as a group-oriented person, embedded in some family, clan, and village, as well as in the world of God.

Honor, a correlation with group identity, serves to solidify the narrative claim that all of Jesus's roles and statuses are ascribed him. Indeed, Jesus enjoys great honor as it was understood by Luke and his audience. No one else in the New Testament is acclaimed "son of the Most High," heir to David's throne, and "my Son, the Beloved." No one else's kingdom was to last for ever and ever. Moreover, all roles ascribed to Jesus are the premier ones known at that time, save that of Caesar. In the early chapters of Luke, Jesus never achieves any honor, because all is ascribed him by the most significant figure known to Luke and his audience. What has Jesus done so that God should say, "with you I am well pleased"?

1. At least for Luke's first four chapters, Jesus is always understood as an individual embedded in some kinship relationship, which provided him with an adequate understanding of himself. He would never be charged with "making himself" anything, as Jesus was in the Fourth Gospel. His complete social identity is provided him either from God, God's angels and prophets, or from his family and kin.

2. In the initial chapters, Luke states that all of Jesus's honorable roles and statuses are ascribed him by a significant other. The **Sender**, who is God, sends various **messages** to different **channels**, all of which identify Jesus in terms of ancestry ("son of David") or in terms of the significant roles he will eventually play ("king" and "savior"). Before Jesus was born and even as an infant, Jesus's ethos is being established by the **Sender**. A person of such distinction deserves to have public voice when an adult.

3. Although most people in the ancient world pursued personal honor and glory, Luke describes Jesus as possessing maximum honor, not because of his own achievements, but because he is ascribed such by one who can enforce its acceptance.

4. The purpose of all of the honor ascribed to Jesus by God was to construct a firm foundation for the ethos of the adult Jesus to act and speak with authority exclusively according to the plan and purpose of God.

CHAPTER 3

An Ethos for Jesus via Status-Elevation Rituals

ONE MORE SOCIAL-SCIENCE MODEL remains to be considered, namely, rituals, either status transformation or confirmation. We focus in this chapter on transformation rituals, and in the next chapter on ceremonies. First of all, Luke narrates nine rituals of Jesus in the first four chapters of his narrative, which, because they are so important to him must also be of significance to us. He does not have a rhetorical template for these, although they were themselves well known events in literature and society. Therefore, modern readers will greatly benefit from careful consideration of them in ways that make sense to us; that is, through examination of them as rituals of transformation and confirmation.

Modern readers are all familiar with the cultural concepts of transformation rituals and ceremonies.[1] Indeed, interest in ritual studies has blossomed recently.[2] In this large field of studies of ritual, we focus solely on the rites that are commonly called status-transformation ones. From cross-cultural comparisons, it is generally agreed that these "occur at crisis points in the life of a group or individual."[3] But the events that are ritual-

---

1. Of immediate use to readers are two articles: McVann, "Rituals of Status Transformation"; Neyrey, "The Foot Washing in John 13:6–11."

2. Other articles can easily open up the terrain for us. First, Uro, "Ritual and Christian Origins," provides a conceptual map of the various directions ritual studies have taken, from early time to the present. DeMaris, "Ritual Studies in the New Testament," does a comparable service for ritual studies explicitly focused on the New Testament.

3. DeMaris, *The New Testament in Its Ritual World*, 21. He cites Grimes, "Defining Nascent Ritual," 550, who defined crucial times that occasion rituals: "One example of ritual time is associated with transformations—changes in social status, seasonal transitions, and crisis moments in histories and life cycles."

ized are not necessarily *crisis* points, and may be familiar changes in social status (marriage and parenthood) or seasonal transitions (menstruation). Ancient authors may not know formal ritual theory or use its jargon, but they narrated the process of very common events such as birth, coming of age, marriage, and death. Luke did also.

We focus on certain passages in Luke (2:6–7, 21, 22–24, 2:41–52; 3:21–22; 4:1–13, 4:15–16, 17–20, and 31–37) in which he narrates different types of events in the life of Jesus. Some are transition markers, such as birth, circumcision, and the like, and others describe the approval or disapproval of the new status claimed. These describe two very different kinds of ritual events, which can be distinguished as status-transformation rituals and ceremonies. Victor Turner described the difference between ritual and ceremony this way: "I consider the term 'ritual' to be more fittingly applied to forms of religious behavior associated with social transitions, while the term 'ceremony' has a closer bearing on religious behavior associated with religious states . . . Ritual is transformative, ceremony confirmatory."[4] In the following diagram, we compare the elements of status-change rituals and ceremonies, which confirm status.[5] The model looks like this.

Transformation Ritual	Characteristic	Confirming Ceremony
1. irregular pauses	Frequency	1. regular pauses
2. unpredictable, when needed	Calendar	2. predictable, planned
3. present-to-future	Temporal focus	3. past-to-present
4. professionals	Presided over by	4. officials
5. change of status, transformation of role or status	Purpose	5. confirmation of status and role

Interpreting this diagram, we learn (1) concerning their **frequency**, both rituals and ceremonies represent pauses in life's rhythms. Certain pauses occur irregularly (sickness, marriage, death), which we call rituals: these are pauses which allow someone to assume new and different roles and statuses. Other pauses, which occur routinely in human lives, we call ceremonies (meals, festivals, birthdays). These do not effect change of role or status, but confirm them. (2) In terms of when they occur on the

---

4. Turner, *The Forest of Symbols*, 95 (italics added); see also Skorupski, *Symbol and Theory*.

5. See Malina, *Christian Origins and Cultural Anthropology*, 139–43. See also Neyrey, *Paul, in Other Words*, 76–80; and McVann, "Rituals of Status Transformation."

calendar, ritual pauses occur unpredictably; we undergo them when necessary. No one plans to be ill or unclean; but when sickness or pollution occur, rituals for changing from those states are handy. Some rituals are unrepeatable status changes, such as birth, coronation, death, and the like. On the other hand, ceremonial pauses, such as Sabbath and Passover, occur on fixed calendar dates. We anticipate and plan for them. (3) In terms of how they **focus time**, ritual pauses take us from present needs to the future, as we change our current status and assume a new role henceforth. Ceremonies, however, look to the past and celebrate its influence on the present. Ceremonies indicate that past roles and statuses continue to exist in the present and influence present social dynamics. (4) Different kinds of people **preside** over rituals and ceremonies. Professionals (e.g., physicians, parents, prophets) preside over or direct status-transformation rituals.[6] But officials (the father at Passover meals, temple priests during worship) preside over or direct the appropriate ceremonies in their institutions.[7] (5) In terms of their **purposes**, ceremonies leave in place the lines of society's maps, because they function to confirm the values and structures of institutions and to celebrate the orderly classification of persons, places, and things in the cosmos.[8] For example, birthdays, annual funeral remembrances, pilgrimage feasts, and the like confirm the roles and statuses of individuals in their own group as well as the group's collective sense of certain holy spaces and holy times that pertain to its festivals.

Ceremonies celebrate the stability of the lines of society's institutions. Conversely, rituals attend precisely to these lines but focus on their crossing. Rituals are stable ways of dealing with necessary instability in the system: boys and girls cross lines to become husbands and wives in a marriage ritual, sick people cross lines and become healthy (Lev 14; Mark 1:44), and sinners become purified (Luke 18:13–14). (The converse is also true: a seemingly innocent person may become guilty through a ritual trial.) The statuses of those who cross lines are thereby changed, and so these rites are

---

6. "Professionals" are particularly trained to preside over rituals of status transformation, whom society authorizes to lead people across lines and boundaries usually judged dangerous. For example, police deal with criminals, doctors, with ill persons, ministers with sinners, and so forth. See Malina, *Christian Origins and Cultural Anthropology*, 144–54.

7. We follow Aristotle's distinction of two basic institutions in antiquity: family/kinship and politics.

8. On "purity systems" and "symbolic universes," see Neyrey, "The Symbolic Universe of Luke–Acts"; and Neyrey, *Paul, in Other Words*, 21–55.

An Ethos for Jesus via Status-Elevation Rituals

called status-transformation rituals. If ceremonies look to the center of the map and the stable lines that make up the map, rituals look to the map's boundaries. These should be stable but may be legitimately or fraudulently crossed.

Status-Elevation Rituals: Prominence

In this chapter we focus only on status-transformation rituals (Luke 2:6–7, 21, 22–24, 2:41–52; 3:21–22), which we will consider as status-*elevation* rituals. Subsequently we can examine other events in the life of Jesus that are best considered ceremonies, which confirm status (4:1–13, 4:15–16, 17–20, and 31–37).

But more needs be said about transformation rituals, because some function to dishonor, negate, and destroy a person's status (e.g., an arrest, a trial, an execution) whereas others serve to enhance honor and status (e.g., an adoption, a vindication from death, an elevation to God's right hand). Because we focus on Luke 1–4, we will first examine the status-elevation rituals repeatedly reported there, which function to establish Jesus as "holy," as one to whom is ascribed the role of Davidic king and even the role of "son of the Most High." For a full appreciation of these rituals, we turn to some anthropological discussion of such.

In terms of theory and modeling, these elevation rituals declare that Jesus should enjoy "prominence."[9] *Prominence* is the antithesis of *deviance*, although both of them refer to being out of place. The word *deviant* labels a person perceived to be negatively out of place—that is, a person who crosses all the lines that make up a orderly or pure world. This is not just a matter of individual acts that transgress norms and customs, but a negative personality trait or quality of personhood. Jesus is described as a *deviant*: "He casts out demons by Beelzebul"; a deviant is one who does not keep the Sabbath or is a false prophet. A deviant does not break rules or laws occasionally but is a lawbreaker or transgressor. In contrast, *prominent* describes a person perceived to be positively out of place. Being positively out of place might result from a new, elevated role or status that is a quality of personhood.[10] Such a person might be labeled a prophet or a king.

---

9. The substance of "Prominence Modelling" may be found in Malina and Neyrey, *Calling Jesus Names*, 93–131.

10. Malina and Neyrey, *Calling Jesus Names*, 40.

In addition to what we have just observed, a status-elevation ritual has several distinctive elements that may help us appreciate it further. Corresponding to the components of a deviance-labeling process, we note five elements of a prominence-labeling ritual. First, we observe agents of approval who promote someone's prominence labeling, such as rule creators, rule enhancers, and prominence-processing agents. Someone other than the person labeled prominent acts on behalf of the one being elevated. In the case of Jesus, God, who is "the Most High . . . God my Savior . . . the Lord God of Israel" is the sole promoter of Jesus's prominence. As the **Sender-of-Senders**, he labels Jesus by means of **channels/messengers** who declare to **recipients** a **message** that consists of official prominence labels, such as "son of the Most High . . . [heir to the] throne of his father David . . . holy, the son of God . . . Savior, who is Christ the Lord . . . the Lord's Christ . . . a light for revelation to the Gentiles, and for glory to thy people Israel . . . redemption of Jerusalem."

As part of this declaration of prominence, lesser figures (**channels**) are needed to enhance the positive label by disseminating it, whom we know of as **messengers**. It is not enough for a monarch to make a decree in the palace about something or someone, because it needs be communicated to the royal subjects (i.e., published). In Luke, angels, such as Gabriel and the angel messenger to the shepherds, bring God's prominent labels of Jesus to individuals and groups. Others "made known what had been told them about this child" (2:17). Male and female prophets continue **channeling the message** of prominence to others (2:25–38).

The second stage of prominence labeling generally consists of making a positive retrospective interpretation of the person so labeled. This, of course, is the task of the Acts of the Apostles, which reconsiders Jesus's death as a deviant in terms of the topos of "noble death."[11] But inasmuch as Luke in chapters 1–2 is writing only the beginning of Jesus's life, there is no fulsome retrospective interpretation of Jesus possible.[12] Luke creates it bit by bit. Moreover, several aspects of Jesus's origins need to be clarified. Jesus will be born to a young woman betrothed but not yet married. This peasant girl will become the spouse of an artisan husband, a landless peasant of a low-status trade. Currently they reside in Nazareth of Galilee, itself a very low-status place. Jesus's origins are hardly auspicious or worthy of prominence. But Luke's narrative tells us that Joseph is a "son of

---

11. Neyrey, *An Encomium for Jesus*, 162–92.
12. Malina and Neyrey, *Calling Jesus Names*, 98–101.

An Ethos for Jesus via Status-Elevation Rituals

David," a member of a very noble clan, who will bring Mary to the royal city of David, Bethlehem, for the birth of Jesus. Although we do not know Mary's tribal affiliation, she has a kinswoman (*suggenis*) who is "a daughter of Aaron" who is married to a member of the priestly "division of Abijah." Mary, then, is at least a "kinswoman" to a member of an exclusive, prominent clan. Independent of the historicity of these data, there is clearly a very positive spin put on the origins of Jesus, which we consider a retrospective interpretation.

Generally when a person is declared a prominent, this labeling might be interpreted as encroaching on the honor status of others.[13] For example, when the *magoi* inquire of Herod, "Where is he who has been born king of the Jews?" (Matt 2:2), Herod "was troubled, and all Jerusalem with him" (Matt 2:3) because of this mortal threat to his sovereignty. But in Luke, the new king is proclaimed as benefit and not threat. Herod does not hear what Gabriel says to Mary, and so is not threatened: "the Lord God will give him the throne of his father David, and he shall reign over the house of David forever" (Luke 1:32–33). This newborn, the angel says, will benefit Israel: "To you is born this day in the city of David a Savior, who is Christ the Lord" (2:11). As noted, Simeon and Anna talk about his benefits, "a light to the Gentiles, and glory to thy people Israel" (2:32) and "the redemption of Jerusalem" (2:28) This prominent person, Jesus, only benefits others.

Luke develops another way of declaring how beneficial is this prominent person, namely, by considering how this person fits in a grand scheme, such as the covenant. We noted this earlier in reference to God "helping his servant Israel, in remembrance of his mercy" (1:54), that is, fulfilling the covenant promise God spoke "to Abraham and his posterity for ever" (1:55). The same, we saw, is said also about John: "to perform the mercy promised to our fathers, and to remember his holy covenant, the oath he swore to our father Abraham" (1:72). This is, moreover, the same covenant of promise that extended through David, of whose throne Jesus is heir. All of this brings benefit on a grand scale.

Therefore all the status-transformation rituals that Jesus—babe, infant, boy, and adult—experiences may properly be considered as status-elevation rituals. They may be understood as indeed bringing transformation

---

13. In cultural anthropology this includes a notion of "zero-sum" materials and an endemic sense of "limited good." See Neyrey and Rohrbaugh, "'He Must Increase, I Must Decrease' (John 3:30)."

but more importantly elevation as well. From the beginning, Jesus is always declared a prominent person, and by the most prominent person, God.

From Fetus to Newborn (Luke 2:6–7)

Let us consider birth as a transformation ritual. Jesus is born just once (John 3:4), and his birth, because a typical pregnancy is calibrated to last nine months, happens at an irregular time: Mary goes into labor when she is ready. Birth is a beginning of a life, which may last thirty or so years; but labor pains quickly become a thing of the past (John 16:21–22). Those presiding over a birth are professionals, such as midwives (and the mother, too); this is what they do on an occasional basis. The purpose of this ritual seems quite obvious: the delivery of a new member into a family and clan.

From Outsider to Insider (Luke 2:21)

Circumcision occurs only once, thank God. While its timing is exact (eight days after birth), its occurrence for the infant boy is irregular, since it depends on when he is born; circumcision can be expected, but it occurs when it is appropriate. Since circumcision is the formal entrance ritual for a male into the covenant, we consider it an elevation which necessarily looks to the future by securing the future status of the new covenant member. Most likely the infant's father performed the circumcision, for which he had scant training or equipment. If he had only one son, he would preside at this ritual only once.[14] It was at this very time that the infant is named, an event that happens only once. Jesus's name, in this case, is dictated from heaven (1:31; 2:21), thus giving it elevated importance.

From Ordinary to Prominent (Luke 2:22–24)

Although the time for the dedication ritual is calibrated as forty days after birth, when that fortieth day occurred depended on the unpredictable day of the infant's birth. The dedication occurs but once in the infant's life, when

---

14. The infant's father (*avi haben*) is commanded to perform the circumcision himself. In modern times, they designate a mohel, a professional specially trained in circumcision and the rituals surrounding the procedure. Under Jewish law, a mohel must draw blood from the circumcision wound.

it is opportune. Since it changes the status of infant from ordinary to consecrated Israelite, it necessarily begins in the present time and secures the future of the infant. The origins of the ritual, moreover, are recorded long ago in Israel's past (Exod 13:1–2). Because most firstborns were dedicated in the villages where they were born, presumably the father presided at the event; Jesus, however, because he was born in Bethlehem, was dedicated in Israel's temple. Moreover, the appropriate sacrificial offering (turtledoves) would have been sacrificed by the priest on duty, not the father. The purpose of the ritual, which happened only once and only to the firstborn son, fulfilled the law whereby the son took on a special relationship to a new Father.

From Peasant to God's Son (Luke 3:21–22)

The event being considered is not Jesus's baptism but what immediately follows it. However scholars construe Jesus's baptism, certain elements in Luke's account must be examined. John, the ritual elder who officiates at the washing rite, is absent from the narrative. And so the Spirit that descends on Jesus has nothing to do with John or John's actions. Moreover, Jesus has been ritually washed, as in preparation for a special event; the washing was only preparatory. Luke says that Jesus was "praying"—that is, in a liminal state and so already in communication with God, who conducts the forthcoming ritual. In Luke, a "holy" Spirit descends on Jesus "like a dove," as Mark and Matthew note, but Luke also says, "in bodily form."[15] When considered in terms of form criticism, the event begins when "the heaven was opened," a not-uncommon marker of a theophany. This theophany features a visual component (*someone* saw the "heavens opened") and an auditory one ("a voice was heard"). Everything thus far is only stage preparation for the ritual transfer of Jesus to a new role and status when the voice speaks, "You are my Son, the Beloved."

This event in the life of Jesus occurred only once, although it was confirmed at his Transfiguration. Its timing was irregular, after Jesus's ritual purification by baptism, when the tableau for the ritual was finally complete. Although the ritual occurs when Jesus was an adult (about thirty years old), it opens for him the beginning of his prophetic life. John the Baptizer, the

---

15. "Like . . ." is a common simile marker in Luke; in the garden, his sweat "became like (*hōsei*) great drops of blood" (22:44); and the Holy Spirit descended on the disciples with "tongues as (*hōsei*) of fire" (Acts 2:3).

conventional figure who presided at baptisms, is no long on the scene; but another figure appears to preside at the transformation, namely, God.

Until this moment, others in Luke's narrative have ascribed to Jesus *sonship* of some sort; while *not* son of Joseph, the baby is son of David and son of the Most High. But now the **Sender** himself sends a new and unique **message** to the adult Jesus, the **recipient**, that officially transforms him into "my Son, the Beloved." This surpasses what was previously ascribed in several ways. Previously, **channels**, such as angels, communicated this message; but now, the **Sender** himself speaks. As honorable as were "son of David" and "son of the Most High," Luke would have us see this new sonship as unique and of highest importance: "my Son, the Beloved, in whom I am well pleased." It might be said that angelic proclamations of sonship were just that, **messages** communicated by **channels** to **recipients** other than Jesus, with no apparent effect on the infant. But God's voice, **Speaker/Sender**, immediately effects now what was only ascribed. Jesus's role and status are different now; as **recipient**, he has received a marker (a **message**) as an adult, and it establishes him immediately for specific tasks, one of which is to have public voice. His days of learning to be an observant son of Israel are over; he moves beyond being just another synagogue participant. Admittedly his status is greatly raised, but exactly what role he will take is still to be decided. Traditionally those anointed with spirit were kings and prophets. And those called "son of God" are generally said to be holy and righteous.[16] Henceforth, Jesus will act upon the pleasure of God, professing a son's loyalty and obedience to this Father. Now, finally, the ethos of Jesus has been established by a Figure who can command the world to respect Jesus' new role and status.[17]

Summary and Conclusions

The social-science models employed in this chapter alert modern readers that the author and the characters narrated in Luke and Acts belong to a culture radically different from that of contemporary readers and their conceptual world. Modern readers are constantly in peril of anachronism and ethnocentrism without these models. The model of a group-oriented

---

16. See Neyrey, *The Passion according to Luke*, 168–70.

17. Not only is it important to recognize events as status elevation rituals, but we need also appreciate the number of them in Luke 1–2 and the function they serve in establishing for Jesus an increasingly worthy ethos.

An Ethos for Jesus via Status-Elevation Rituals

personality makes all the more important the fact that all of Jesus's roles and statuses are ascribed him by higher-ranking persons.[18] He does not vaingloriously claim them; he depends on others to tell him who he is. Thus the **Sender** and all of his **channels/mediators** are necessarily shaping Jesus's ethos. It is never his task to do this himself.

Those who know what ancient honor was and its importance can greatly appreciate the honorable persons who act to honor Jesus. What they have to say about him, moreover, is exceptionally honorable: for instance they assign him the role of king or son of the Most High or Savior of Israel. It matters, moreover, that these honorific roles and statuses keep accumulating, suggesting that the future honor of this person increases immensely, and will only keep growing. Not to know about honor in the ancient world is to lack appreciation of the most precious thing that Jesus's peers can give him.

Therefore all the status-transformation rituals that Jesus—babe, infant, boy, and adult—experiences may properly be considered as status-elevation rituals. They may be understood as indeed bringing transformation but more importantly elevation as well. From the beginning, Jesus is always declared a prominent person, and by a most prominent person, God. In the next chapter, we will consider the confirmatory ceremonies that Jesus experiences in Luke 1–4.

What, then, do we know when we know all of this? What conclusions might we draw?

1. It matters if readers know communication theory, for they are then aware of the significance of the steps and stages of any communication. It matters **who** speaks a **message** to **whom**, via what **channel/mediator**, and for what **purpose**. It matters that in Luke's narrative the premier and only **Sender** is God, who, generally employs **channels** (angels, prophets), to tell only certain **recipients** a **message** about his own "son." We know, moreover, Luke's rhetorical **purpose** in narrating this communication, namely, to establish a proper ethos for Jesus ultimately to enjoy public voice.

2. Group-oriented persons, such as Jesus and all others who populate the world of the New Testament, are dependent on their kin, village, and *ethnos*, to tell them who they are. Determinations of who they are do

---

18. Unlike the typical accusations made in John, Jesus never "makes himself" anything (see John 5:18; 8:53; 10:33; 19:7, 12).

not come through personal choices but through claims of honor and worth, which can only be made by worthy and honorable persons on another's behalf, and which must then be validated in the eyes and ears of those who hear them.

3. All the honorable name-calling of Jesus in Luke 1–2 is done by worthy persons, who have sufficient honor standing to make claims on behalf of Jesus. The meaning of honor in Jesus's world and its choreography serve to provide Jesus with a most significant human status in order to establish him as a person who deserves to be heard. This is done by worthy ascription to him of names, titles, and roles that are of recognized high status. An honorable person must be born in an honorable place, of honorable parents and ancestors; this person's claims to honor, moreover, must be made in public and attested to in public. The status of the one ascribing honor determines the quality of donation of honor.

4. Status-transformation rituals regularly occurred in the world of Luke and Jesus. Any time a new role and status is ascribed to Jesus, it is narrated in familiar terms, with appropriate persons officiating and acting in familiar ways in order to make evident the transition. Birth, circumcision, naming, and dedication are such moments. Similarly, they are presided over by persons respected for their ability to manage the rituals properly. John, himself a prophetic figure, presides over a ritual that effects change of status, namely, from sinner to purified. How much more significant, then, is the transformation ritual signaled by the heavens opening and the Spirit descending to accompany the ascription of very high role and status to Jesus.

5. We count four transformation rituals and five ceremonies narrated in Luke 1–4. Although different, they collectively argue for the exalted role and status of Jesus. A sequence such as this had a rhetorical name: the sequence is called a *klimax*.[19]

6. The very fact that Luke spends so much time on the origins of Jesus (chapters 1–2) itself indicates Luke's awareness of his need to establish a proper ethos for Jesus. Nothing concerning honorable origins is left out; every traditional way of honoring a worthy person by narrating his origins is included.

---

19. The Greeks call it *klimax*, the Romans, *graditio*. See Lausberg, *Handbook of Literary Rhetoric*, 279 (# 623).

An Ethos for Jesus via Status-Elevation Rituals

7. But Luke also narrates that Jesus experienced ceremonies, whose narrative purpose was to confirm Jesus in a certain role and status. A ceremony celebrates an event in the past whose effect exists even in the present and will continue into the future. Thus, every time Jesus attends synagogue on the Sabbath, as was his custom, and every time he teaches or speaks, which became customary, the warrant for his public voice is confirmed again and again.

CHAPTER 4

Confirming Jesus's Role and Status with Ceremonies

Besides rituals of status elevation, Luke's audience hears about ceremonies that confirm the new status and roles ascribed Jesus. Some occur in Jesus's early years (2:41–52) and others when, as a mature adult, he began to exercise his public voice (4:1–13, 15–16, 17–20, and 31–37). As noted, not all transformations occur when Jesus is a babe or infant; for instance, Jesus is an adult at the theophany at the Jordan when he is declared "my Son, the Beloved." And not all ceremonies are to be found in the adult life of Jesus. Two ceremonies in particular attest to Jesus's observance of important rituals in the life of the house of Israel—Passover and attendance at the local synagogue on the Sabbath. His regular participation in both indicate that Jesus was trained to be an observant Israelite, an essential element in his ethos.

Traditional Ceremonies

Passover Every Year in Jerusalem (2:41–52)

Ceremonies consist of the same elements as transformation rituals, but in very different dress. Passover, the premier ceremony of Israel, occurred on a fixed calendar date: in the beginning month of the year, on the fourteenth day of Nisan, during the full moon; it was an annual festival, precisely calculated according to the fullness of the moon, which rises after the vernal equinox. As a most significant feast, it was predictable and planned with

Confirming Jesus's Role and Status with Ceremonies

great exactitude.¹ It recalled the exodus from Egypt, bringing that ancient passover from slavery to freedom into the present.² Inasmuch as it was a kinship festival, it was presided over by the father of the family, who slaughtered and cooked the lamb. It functioned, like all ceremonies, to confirm membership in the house of Israel, and to keep in memory the foundation narrative of Israel. And so, Luke says, "[Jesus's] parents went to Jerusalem every year at the feast of Passover" (2:41). Although Luke does not mention any Passover feast after the return to Nazareth (2:51), he expects his audience to think that Jesus and family celebrated Passover annually, whether in Jerusalem or Nazareth.

The Passover pilgrimage in Luke 2:41-52 suffers a significant disturbance by the son, Jesus, when he breaks many conventions at the end of the feast. First, he remains in Jerusalem, separating himself from his family; second, he engages in activity unsuitable for a twelve-year-old when he performs as a precocious child listening and asking questions of adult males³ not of his kinship group. As a twelve-year-old boy, he owes his parents obedience; but he is conflicted because he has two fathers and cannot decide which father he should obey. No child, moreover, should ever address a parent in the surly tones that he does: they reproach him ("Why have you treated us like this?"), and he answers their question with a question ("Did you not know that I must be in my Father's house?"). Answering a question with a question is very aggressive.⁴ In this encounter, many things are unceremoniously upset in this fixed kinship ceremony. Eventually, they are

---

1. Passover was the crown jewel of pilgrimage festivals: "Three times a year all your males shall appear before the LORD your God at the place that he will choose: at the festival of unleavened bread, at the festival of weeks, and at the festival of booths" (Deut 16:16).

2. On the political significance of this feast in the time of Jesus, see Oakman, *The Political Aims of Jesus*, 94-97, 104.

3. It is one thing to listen to the male elders of one's kinship group, but quite another thing to exercise public voice in a different institution (political) about matters beyond one's upbringing. Moreover, as we read Luke 2:44-45 more closely, Jesus was among neither the adult males nor the adult females of his kinship group; after a day's journey, when the family units gathered back together, Jesus was not present, although it took all day for his mother to realize that she did not find him among the females; nor did his father locate him among the males. Jesus, then, was in transition between being a boy, who might be found among either males or females, and being a young man. Thus, he was absent from his kinship group, but oddly present in the political institution. The story itself solves the problem: he is not yet a male adult in any sense, and he returns where he belongs, his kinship group.

4. Neyrey, "Questions, *Chreiai*, and Challenges to Honor."

all put back in proper place when the pilgrimage ends as it should: "Then he went down with them and came to Nazareth, and was obedient to them" (2:51). The kinship institution is now confirmed: right place, right parents, right behavior.

Ceremonies in Luke 3–4

Confirmation of Sonship (4:1–13)

We saw earlier that Jesus experiences a status elevation when God ascribes to him an impressive role and status (3:21–22). Jesus is ritually made a prominent when God adopts him and addresses him, "My son, the Beloved." But Luke's audience is not surprised to learn that this role and status must be confirmed by a ceremony we call the "testing" of Jesus.[5] It matters greatly, moreover, whether we read 4:1–13 as a testing or a temptation.[6]

Scholars agree that the episode narrated in 4:1–13 is related to what preceded it in 3:21–22, "an aftermath to the baptismal identification and anointing."[7] Many note its connection to what follows, "a major prelude to his ministry."[8] But we wish to consider 4:1–13 as a ceremony that confirms the status transformation accomplished by God in 3:21–22. Although it occurs forty days after his desert sojourn, the number of days here communicates only a fixed and traditional period of preparation, not a calendar date. Moreover, Luke and his audience know of many such traditional periods of preparation, which argues that such events are a common occurrence in the preparation of the careers of Israel's prophets. And, the temporal

---

5. Most treatments of 4:1–13 have focused on the historicity of the event, its place in the handing on of traditions, and other traditional questions. But rarely do we find comment on its literary genre or characteristics. One such comment was made in Johnson, *The Gospel of Luke*, 75–76: "No more need be said about the threefold structure of the story except that it is typically folkloric, and that it is ominously echoed by the threefold betrayal by Peter in 22:54–62 and the threefold taunting of Jesus at the Cross (23:35, 37, 39)." But authors familiar with rhetoric and the genre chreia will see much more here.

6. Temptation or testing? A "testing" looks to confirmation, while "tempting" implies that status might indeed be changed. While the verb *peirazō* may mean "to tempt," as in "to seduce" (Gal 6:1; 1 Cor 7:5), its basic meaning is "to discover the nature or character of something, . . . put to the test" (BDAG 792–93). While it is tempting to interpret 4:1–13 in terms of Satan's tempting of Adam in Gen 3, this comparison wilts when all of the testings are viewed.

7. Nolland, *Luke 1—9:20*, 178.

8. Bock, *Luke 1:1—9:50*, 363.

Confirming Jesus's Role and Status with Ceremonies

perspective brings the past (theophany commissioning) into the present, and so allows that transformation of Jesus to extend into his future behavior, which is how ceremonies function. The purpose of the testing manifests that the honor ascribed to Jesus by God is worthily secure.[9] Jesus will demonstrate—to the audience, at least—that he is authentically "[God's] Son, the Beloved, with whom [God is] well pleased."

Jesus, son of God, is the central figure in 4:1–13, but two other figures are present: the Spirit of God and the devil. First, God's Spirit has been attached to Jesus since the theophany: (1) "the Holy Spirit descended upon him in bodily form" (3:21); (2) "Jesus, full of the Holy Spirit . . . was led by the Spirit" (4:1); and so "Spirit" functions as Jesus's mentor and support. The other figure, the devil, only now appears on the scene and quickly leaves,[10] and his role is that of the "tester," who would challenge Jesus so as to make void the role ascribed him at the theophany. Luke presumes that we presume that the Spirit of God remained beside Jesus.

The ceremonial dynamics described in 4:1–13 should be considered in the light of another progymnastic genre, the chreia.[11] This genre, which expresses the choreography of all of the challenge/riposte exchanges in the Gospels, contains certain predictable steps: (1) a man renowned for wisdom or virtue, (2) is attacked by an opponent, who (3) asks the wise man challenging questions, (4) for the purpose of defeating, dishonoring, and dethroning the wise man, and (5) to whom the wise man must respond adroitly and so put the challenger to flight. Whereas in typical chreiai

---

9. Modern readers are all too familiar with "testing" as confirmation. Every physician must be board certified, even many times, depending on the specialization in question; every lawyer, at least in the US, must pass the bar exam to be licensed to practice; the same is true of the certification exam for accountants. These exams, then, confirm the legitimacy of previous training.

10. Although the antagonist is "the devil," his legions will remain on the scene to battle Jesus in the form of "unclean spirits" causing disease and illness. Luke, to be sure, implies that Jesus always acts by the direction of and with the power of God's Spirit, and so acts as God's champion (cf. 11:15–22). Thus, we find in Luke an extended series of encounters of Jesus with unclean spirits (4:33, 36; 6:18; 7:21; 8:2; 9:42; 11:24; and 13:11). Jesus's association with God's Spirit, however, goes back to Luke's initial remark from Gabriel that Jesus's physical being will be caused by God's action through the Holy Spirit: "The Holy Spirit will come upon you and the power of the Most High will overshadow you" (1:35) the same Holy Spirit enlightened Simeon twice (2:25, 26) to acclaim Jesus; and John declared that Jesus would "baptize [with] the Holy Spirit and fire" (3:16). The same Spirit filled Jesus before his "testing" and empowered him when he returned to Galilee (4:1, 14).

11. Neyrey, "Questions, *Chreiai*, and Challenges to Honor."

challenging questions are asked in distinct or separate testings, 4:1–13 is structured with three successive questions of the same ilk. And, whereas the nub of a challenge in a chreia might range over many topics and subjects, the challenge to Jesus focuses on one point: "If you are the son of God . . ." The issue, then, is as much one of loyalty and virtue (justice) as it is of wisdom.

Challenge	Riposte
"If you are the Son of God, command these stones to become bread."	Jesus answered him, "It is written, 'One does not live by bread alone.'"
"To you I will give their glory and all this authority; for it has been given over to me, and I will give it to anyone I please. If you, then, will worship me, it will all be yours."	Jesus answered him, "It is written 'Worship the Lord your God, and serve only him.'"
"If you are the Son of God, throw yourself down from here, for it is written 'He will command his angels concerning you, to protect you.'"	Jesus answered him, "It is said, 'Do not put the Lord your God to the test.'"

Indeed, filial obedience is fully displayed and so Jesus's role of son is confirmed.[12] But, because Jesus answers each testing with an appropriate citation from Deuteronomy, he is portrayed as displaying wisdom or learning. When later he argues from the Scriptures, it has already been demonstrated that he is adept in reading the Bible. Almost all chreiai occur in public, probably in the synagogue or the agora. This matters, because all honor challenges and ripostes require some audience to give a verdict to the contest: Who won? Who lost? God's Holy Spirit saw the entire contest, and so can report to God the success of Jesus, "my Son, the Beloved." He can also report that the challenger was chased from the field. Luke's very audience, of course, is the designated audience who assesses Jesus's resounding riposte.

More can be said about 4:1–13 when it is examined as a rhetorical chreia.[13] First, it casts the testing in a rhetorical form with which Luke's audience was familiar, a genre appropriate to describe conflict and challenge. A chreia equals a challenge. It matters not if three challenges are stitched

---

12. See Thompson, "Called—Proved—Obedient."

13. In addition to the literature about the genre chreia noted elsewhere in this monograph, see Hock, trans. and ed., *The Chreia in Ancient Rhetoric*; Mack and Robbins, *Patterns of Persuasion*.

Confirming Jesus's Role and Status with Ceremonies

into one, for this intensifies the challenge, and so too the riposte. Second, inasmuch as chreiai report on the testing of the wisdom or virtue of an honorable man, the chreia genre here also serves to confirm the acumen of Jesus to teach and to act with virtue. Third, because this chreia is part of the initial presentation of Jesus here, it schools Luke's audience to be familiar with repeated and similar challenges to Jesus throughout the narrative, told in the same rhetorical pattern. We argue, moreover, that a chreia displays ritualized conflict. Furthermore, while it might seem that status is attacked, with the possibility of defeat and so change of status, the chreia genre is a stylized way of describing the defense of role and status by the protagonist. He always wins, for such is the nature of this rhetorical form. Therefore, a challenge/riposte exchange is a chreia, which dramatizes ritual conflict in a stereotypical manner, and this stereotypical conflict can be considered a ceremony. In regard to 4:1-13, we may say, then, that testings are in fact chreiai/challenges that are ritualized ceremonies that serve to confirm the superiority of Jesus, "[God's] Son, the Beloved."

A Confirmation Ceremony (4:14-15)

Now, as Jesus steps upon his proper stage,[14] Luke's audience knows of Jesus's role and status. And so also do the narrative characters in the story: "A report about him spread through all the surrounding country." But more is said: "He taught in their synagogues." The first remark, "a report . . . through all the surrounding country," serves as an honor claim for Jesus, a claim that is ceremoniously confirmed. The second remark, "he taught in their synagogues," also confirms the report about him, even to the point that he is allowed to speak a particular word to a recognized audience on a distinctive occasion: in the synagogue on the Sabbath. "Praised by everyone," he is confirmed in his role and status. Jesus's reputation presumes that he had already spoken publicly, most likely in synagogues on Sabbath; thus, a report about him had arisen and spread. On fixed and predictable occasions,

---

14. Much confusion surrounds how commentators understand what occurs in 4:14-15. For some it is merely a change of geography, i.e. a "return to Galilee," whereas others call attention to the role of the "spirit," such as Fitzmyer, *The Gospel according to Luke I-IX*, 522. Nolland rightly points in a profitable direction, when he says, "V 14a introduces Jesus' public ministry in Galilee as bursting on the scene as a culmination of his baptismal anointing with the Spirit" (*Luke 1—9:20*, 187). And while 4:14-15 might serve as a "generalizing introduction to the accounts of concrete ministry in Nazareth and Capernaum," closer attention must be paid to the details narrated.

then, he acted regularly in an approved role that was commonly recognized. Luke's readers appreciate that the event in the past, the theophany, legitimates the present behavior of Jesus. As we are told, he "taught in their synagogues," in more than one synagogue on more than one Sabbath. Each synagogue was presided over by an official, "the chief of the synagogue" (*archisynagogos*), who in each gathering presumably allows Jesus to have public voice. And now throughout Galilee Jesus is confirmed in his role and status, which is what should happen in true ceremonies. To describe Jesus's early teaching in synagogues as his introduction is too weak a label here, for this is foremost a *performance*, that is, a ceremony.

A Ceremony within a Ceremony (4:16-30)

Although Luke mentions in passing that Jesus had already begun to teach in synagogues on the Sabbath—in Capernaum, to be precise—the episode in the Nazareth synagogue is generally considered in important ways to be the first and therefore the prototypical story of Jesus, probably because of its length.[15] Luke considers it a genuine ceremony that he is narrating here. The temporal occasion is clear: "He went into the synagogue . . . on the Sabbath." Not only are synagogue services themselves regular and predictable ceremonies, but Jesus's attendance is likewise, "as was his custom." We underscore this temporal factor for what it evidently implies: the very fact that Jesus now stands up to read presumes that something in the past ("a report concerning him went out throughout all the surrounding country") warrants Jesus's present actions. Moreover, when Jesus reads Isaiah, he declares that past is now present: "Today this Scripture . . ." Moreover, Luke presumes that his audience is adequately familiar with the regular parts of a Sabbath service, which is typical in Luke's high-context world. The typical synagogue ceremony features many regular parts, such as the prayers (the Shema and Amidah), readings from the Law and the Prophets, and possibly a homily based on his reading of Isa 61:1. Although Luke does not mention an official, we know (as mentioned earlier) that synagogue meetings were conducted by an *archisynagogos*, who presumably authorized

---

15. Most of the literature on Luke 4:16-29 considers basically the important issues of source and historicity. But it seems that only scholars with training in literary matters appreciate its rhetorical position and function. See Combrink, "The Structure and Significance of Luke 4:16-30"; Anderson, "Broadening Horizons"; Hill, "Rejection of Jesus at Nazareth (Luke 4:16-30)."

Confirming Jesus's Role and Status with Ceremonies

Jesus to speak. It is asking too much to presume that Jesus simply stood up and asked to read. The purpose of synagogue meetings is to confirm membership in the house of Israel by praying conventional Israelite prayers and hearing its Scriptures. Thus far, a ceremony is apparent in a synagogue meeting both in its structural parts and in the roles described.

But something breaks the structure of the ceremony, or so it seems. A conflict erupts in the reaction to Jesus's honor claims by his peers in the Nazareth synagogue. If confirmation of solidarity is the aim of a synagogue ceremony, that appears to be broken by conflict. How, then, to assess this conflict? As we saw earlier, the progymnastic genre chreia functions to ritualize conflict. Conflict is endemic in the ancient world and was conducted in physical encounters, as well as narrative ones. The singular way to present a narrative account of conflict was to cast it in the form of a chreia. As we argued, a chreia is itself a ceremony, a conventional series of steps that function to confirm the wisdom and prowess of an honorable man.

Let us read the part of the meeting in Nazareth's synagogue in which events are narrated according to the rhetorical genre suited to dramatizing conflict, namely, the rhetorical genre chreia. At first, this chreia does not seem to have a temporal fixity; it may occur anytime, but as we shall see in the subsequent stories about Jesus, it generally occurs during a synagogue meeting. Thus, it does have a fixed time, a synagogue service on the Sabbath. As in all ceremonies, its sequential steps are conventional and familiar. As shown above, a protagonist is presented, known for prowess of some sort. In Nazareth, Jesus's reputation for prophetic healing precedes him: "What we have heard you did at Capernaum, do here also in your own country" (4:23). Thus, Jesus arrives in Nazareth with an honor claim, namely, his reputation. As protagonist, Jesus plays the role in a typical chreia of a wise or noble person whose reputation is well-known. While Jesus's reputation grounds his initial honor claim, he proceeds to make a new and superior one, both in his presumed worthiness to read the prophet Isaiah and in his boldness to declare that Isaiah spoke about Jesus himself. He is, after all, a landless artisan peasant, for whom such a claim would sound outrageous. Conflict is inevitable. The fuse is lit.

Although modern readers are familiar with the form and dynamics of the rhetorical chreia, it is unlikely that they appreciate the cultural background needed to understand it. In Luke's high-context world, people generally perceived the world in terms of a social perception of *limited good*. This means that all things in the world (land, goods, and even honor) were limited in supply; there simply was no way to grow them. For Luke's characters and audience it necessarily followed that all social interactions occurred in terms of a *zero-sum game*. If Jesus appears to rise above his birth status, those in the synagogue will interpret this as his attempt to increase his honor, which can only happen if theirs diminishes.[16] Conflict is inevitable. But, at first Luke narrates no challenge to Jesus's claims, reporting that "all spoke well of him and were amazed at the gracious words that came from his mouth" (4:22). But the fuse is burning down.

The Nazareth synagogue quickly appreciates the threat of Jesus's claims. As night follows day, they realize that Jesus's claims are insulting, offensive, and belittling. In a world of limited good, he is claiming increase in honor, which means that their standing is diminished. He must be challenged. Aware of the chreia, Luke's audience perceives the specific challenges, which are pointed attacks on the protagonist. Luke, moreover, narrates these challenges in their typical rhetorical form (i.e., a question). Given Jesus's low birth status, the Nazareth synagogue appears to mount its attack precisely on this point. Who is this pretender? What is this vainglory? What Luke reports is a conventional attack on Jesus's generational origins: how dare a peasant artisan make such claims: "Is not this Joseph's son?" (4:22).

Jesus must make a riposte to their challenge, which seems to include many items that express their challenge but are turned into a riposte. If healings in Nazareth such as he did in Capernaum is the issue, then he surfaces that challenge with the maxim: "Doctor, heal yourself" (4:23, my trans.). Jesus's riposte takes a more aggressive turn, as he speaks another maxim: "No prophet is accepted in the prophet's hometown" (4:24). Where, then, should a prophet perform? Exclusively at home, or elsewhere? But Jesus is hardly the first prophet to perform good deeds elsewhere than in his own home; in riposte Jesus cites the examples of Elijah and Elisha as a proper defense for his own actions. The success of Jesus's riposte to the challenges from his fellow worshipers is narrated with a renewed challenge from the Nazareth synagogue. In a chreia, the challengers would typically be silenced or forced from the field, but here their challenge only increases, and takes a murderous turn: "They got up, drove him out of the town, and led him to the brow of the hill on which their town was built, so that they

---

16. These two anthropological concepts are discussed in Neyrey and Rohrbaugh, "'He Must Increase, I Must Decrease' (John 3:30)." See also Malina, *New Testament World* (3rd ed.), 81–107.

might hurl him off the cliff" (4:29). But Jesus deflects this ultimate challenge: "But he passed through the midst of them and went on his way" (4:30).

Therefore, we observe how Luke uses the genre chreia to narrate the conflict in 4:16–30. Moreover, the chreia is itself a ceremony with conventional parts sequentially narrated. If ceremonies function to confirm someone in a role or status, then this chreia confirms Jesus as a successful protagonist in this stylized conflict. Thus, we argue that the synagogue service in Nazareth is itself a ceremony, and that the conflict that erupts in it is told in ceremonial fashion as a chreia. After all, a typical chreia is itself a ceremony. Moreover, when Jesus's claim to be an authentic prophet is rejected, Luke's audience understands that even the very rejection of the claim is another claim to status: "No prophet is accepted in the prophet's hometown." So, rejection of honor claim is itself a claim to the role and status of a prophet.

But as Luke's narrative both in the Gospel and Acts continues, we find much data suggesting that the conflict described there is common, if not a usual element of a synagogue service. The evidence for this comes from a study of the typical ceremonial structure of a synagogue meeting according to Luke's Gospel and Acts. What did Luke the author know about the regular sequence of events in a typical service? What did he presume his audience knew? As an accomplished writer, Luke must assume that what he says makes some sense to his audience. There must be some common understanding by author and audience about a typical synagogue service, indeed, ceremony.

Excursus: What Happens in a Typical Synagogue Meeting?

Jesus attends the synagogue every Sabbath, "as was his custom"; indeed, six times Luke narrates that Jesus himself attended a synagogue on the Sabbath. To describe what a synagogue service might look like in Luke's Gospel, we have culled and synthesized remarks scattered in his Gospel and especially in Acts.[17] As a considerate author, Luke instructs his audience about the typical events that constitute a conventional synagogue meeting.

---

17. A full treatment of the synagogue and its service deserves at least one volume. But, inasmuch as our focus rests on Luke (Gospel and Acts), it seems sufficient to see

1. The synagogue is a meeting itself or a place of meeting, where only adult Israelite males gather to confirm their identity as Israelites who worship God.

2. Each synagogue hosts the male population of a village, although Acts indicates that Israelites of different language groups and social statuses might also gather together (Acts 6:9). Members of a village synagogue, then, would have significant social information about each member.

3. An *archisynagogos* officiated at the meeting (Luke 8:49; 13:14; Acts 18:8, 17), although according to Acts there might be several heads of the synagogue officiating at a single meeting (13:15). As part of his officiating, he deputizes others either to read or to deliver a word of exhortation. He might even act as a judge. Apparently, there was a seating arrangement that allowed socially prominent people to have "seats of honor": "Woe to you Pharisees! For you love to have the seat of honor in the synagogues" (Luke 11:43). A form of hierarchical seating, then, seems to be common.

4. The service consisted of prayers (the Shema and the Amidah), as well as readings from the Scriptures: "After the reading of the law and the prophets..." (Luke 4:17–19; Acts 13:15). From sources other than Luke and Acts, we know that a "homily" was preached.[18] Jesus's remarks after reading the scroll of Isaiah suggest that he gave an interpretation (also known as a homily) on that passage of Scripture, Isa 61:1.

5. We find many, many references to debates and controversies occurring during synagogue meetings. The terminology used for these is not consistent: *dialegomai, dialogizomai, dialogismos,* and *suzēteō*.[19] And while these terms might describe intense discussions, the context in which they appear suggests something more severe—that is, controversy and argument. For example, Stephen finds himself in a controversy that proves deadly: "Then some of those who belonged to the synagogue of the Freedmen (as it was called)..., stood up and argued (*suzētountes*) with Stephen" (Acts 6:9). Many of Paul's encounters in Greek synagogues may start out neutrally, but often conclude with attacks on him. For example, at Thessalonika, "Paul

---

what Luke says and what his audience might already know or learn from Luke's treatment. Incomplete, but sufficient for this monograph.

18. Wills, "The Form of the Sermon"; Black, "The Rhetorical Form."

19. In both his gospel and Acts, Luke reports much argument and debate (according to BDAG 232); *dialegomai,* "converse with/discuss," "argue" (Acts 17:2; 18:4, 19; 19:8–9; 20:7; 24:12, 25); *dialogizomai,* "consider carefully, discuss" (Luke 1:29; 3:15; 12:17; 24:38; *dialogismos,* "verbal exchange when conflicting ideas are expressed" (Luke 5:21–22; 6:8; 9:46–47).

went in, as was his custom, and for three weeks he argued with them from the Scriptures, explaining and proving that it was necessary for the Christ to suffer and to rise from the dead" (Acts 17:3). Opponents arose, which caused Paul and Silas to be sent away at night (Acts 17:9). It will always be a commentator's decision whether to translate *dialegomai* and *dialogizomai* neutrally as "discuss" or aggressively as "argue." Paul, never willing to miss an opportunity, seems regularly to enter the local synagogue upon arrival there (Acts 18:4, 19; 19:8).[20] He is not a conciliatory speaker.

6. Synagogues also appear to have been places where judgment was delivered and even chastisement rendered. Paul himself sought and received judicial authority to enter synagogues and "arrest" believers: "Saul, still breathing threats and murder against the disciples of the Lord, went to the high priest and asked him for letters to the synagogues of Damascus, so that if he found any belonging to the Way, he might bring them bound to Jerusalem" (Acts 9:2). This presumes some sort of trial in the synagogue, where accusations would be made and testimony given. Saul acted like a judge who declared some innocent and others guilty; if guilty, they were "bound" and taken to Jerusalem, for unspecified punishments. In some cases, Paul did not wait for a Jerusalem trial, as he himself said: "in every synagogue I imprisoned and beat those who believed in you" (Acts 22:19). While we are not certain where Paul was when he himself was disciplined, he says that it happened often: "Five times I have received at the hands of the Jews the forty lashes less one ... Once I received a stoning" (2 Cor 11:24–25). A synagogue would seem a likely place for this public shaming. When appropriate, therefore, a synagogue could become an arena of judgment, even one where chastisement was administered.

We benefit from this by learning what Luke says might take place in a synagogue because it demonstrates that synagogue services might regularly have ceremonial parts such as debates and arguments, as well as judgment and chastisement. Conflict, moreover, was not alien to its meeting. In short, much evidence in Luke–Acts indicates that these two elements—arguments and judgments—were conventional parts of the typical synagogue meeting. Thus, they belong in the sequence of conventional steps that constitute a

---

20. In Acts 24:12, Paul "cheerfully made my defense" before the Jewish elite and the governor. He emphatically states that, upon his return to Jerusalem, "they did not find me disputing with anyone or stirring up a crowd, either in the temple or in the synagogues." It would appear that Paul is denying that he acted in Jerusalem as he was wont to do regularly in other synagogues. Paul, himself a controversial person, seemed prone to cause controversy.

synagogue meeting as a ceremony. They are themselves ceremonies—ceremonies within a ceremony.

The narrative in Luke 4:16–30, therefore, presumes that Luke's audience would have some familiarity with the parts of a Sabbath synagogue service, many of which are highlighted in the Nazareth meeting. Moreover, we argue that conflict (debate, controversy) was also a regular part of a typical service. Luke narrates it according to the genre chreia, which we know to be a ritualized form of conflict, itself a ceremony. Thus, the overall narrative in 4:16–29 is a ceremony, and the conflict part is likewise a ceremony. And so, we find a specific ceremony contained within a broader ceremony.

༄ ༄ ༄

More Ceremonial Conflict in a Synagogue (4:31–37)

The Nazareth synagogue meeting, however, is not the sole example of how conflict might appear as a regular part of a synagogue meeting. Luke narrates two more synagogue meetings that include or feature conflict, although we have space here only to consider the first one. After Nazareth, Jesus "went down to Capernaum," which previously served as the provocation for the conflict in Nazareth ("'do here also in your home town the things that we have heard you did at Capernaum'" [4:23]). A ceremony occurs in its synagogue on the Sabbath, and all appears to go well. Jesus acts in his ceremonial role ("and [he] was teaching them on the sabbath" [4:31]), which the hearers confirm ("They were astounded at his teaching" [4:32]). But a conflict arises, which might also be a ceremonial part of a synagogue service, narrated in the form of a chreia, which is characterized by challenge and riposte. When the confrontation begins, Jesus has already been acknowledged as a wise and powerful person. But, just as in typical chreiai an antagonist challenges a man of honor, so now an "unclean demon" attacks Jesus. It assuredly is an attack and challenge for two reasons. First, the demon "cried out with a loud voice" (4:33), giving a shout or call to action, not a civil address. Second, the demon himself declares that they are mortal enemies: "What have you to do with us, Jesus of Nazareth? Have you come to destroy us?" (4:34).[21] Just as Luke narrates that the demon in 4:1–12 hid

21. As in military combat, the prowess of an opponent serves to increase the honor of the person attacked. It is one thing for mortals such as "scribes and Pharisees" to attack Jesus, but quite another when the antagonist belongs to another grade of opponent. Thus Jesus is challenged by a significant foe, an "unclean demon" whom Luke's audience would

Confirming Jesus's Role and Status with Ceremonies

his poison and practiced deception, so also let us suspect that this demon's first remarks conceal a trap.

Four things in 4:34a need closer examination: (1) the boisterous cry, (2) the (hostile) questions, (3) the admission of mortal combat, and (4) the address of Jesus by his personal name. Why put Jesus on guard? Why not lodge a sneak attack? Is the demon seeking some advantage? But what? If the first testing between Satan and Jesus (4:1–13) was private, this is public, before all in the synagogue, which means that Jesus's failure will be evident in the eyes of all. First, "crying out with a loud voice" itself issues a challenge. Second, typical of chreiai, the antagonist makes his challenge in the form of hostile questions, in this case, two questions. They are prefaced with a kind of mockery, "Ha!" The demon concedes the gravity of the combat, asking if Jesus has "come to destroy us" (4:34) Here the demon exaggerates, because in 4:13 the devil withdraws until an opportune time to renew testing, and Luke records many more attacks by demons (4:41; 8:27–38; 9:1, 42; 10:17; 13:32; 22:3, 31). While the demon's hyperbole in 4:34 heightens the level of combat, it must be examined.

Second, Luke would have his audience connect the testing in 4:1–13 with this one. Although Luke concludes that testing in 4:13 with the remark that "When the devil ended every temptation, he departed from him until an opportune time," now a demon is back onstage, continuing the earlier line of attack. Demons, it would seem, are hard to destroy. Does the demon here give up any ground by stating, "What have you to do with us . . . Have you come to destroy us" (4:34)? As in 4:1–13, is there a deception here; is a poison coated sweetly? The demon's remark seems to cede much: Jesus is the protagonist and demon is the antagonist. Nothing seems hidden in the demon's acknowledgment of conflicting powers. But then deception and trickery are indeed hidden in the devil's conversation with Jesus in 4:1–12. Does this demon really envision defeat? If so, then why provoke this contest? Such a victory does not occur in 4:1–13, nor will it occur here or in any other challenge/riposte. Combat with demons continues (4:41; 8:27–38; 9:1, 42; 10:17; 13:32; 22:3, 31). What advantage might this demon gain by his questioning? Even as he seems to concede something to Jesus, what might accrue to him in return?

Third, is some gambit made in the demon's questions? The questions are hostile in themselves, but is any poison or trap hidden when the demon addresses Jesus by his personal name, "Jesus of Nazareth"? What would

---

understand to be among the ranks of Beelzebul.

Luke's audience make of the demon using form of address? What cultural background is needed to understand this kind of speech? To begin with, what does it mean to address a person by his personal name? Twice in Luke a demon addresses Jesus by his personal name.

> "What have you to do with us, *Jesus of Nazareth*?" (4:34)
> "What have you to do with me, *Jesus, Son of the Most High God*?" (8:28)

But what were the cultural implications of addressing a person by his personal name?[22] Addressing a person by his personal name implies a certain relationship,[23] either peer to peer or superior to inferior; it speaks to status, and so to power. Although God ascribes Jesus his name (1:31; 2:21), God never addresses Jesus by it. But two other groups do: demons (4:34; 8:28) and petitioners (17:13; 18:37–38; 23:42). Usages of his personal name by both groups, when considered in cultural terms, express some claim on Jesus.

When petitioners address someone, they confront him with a challenge of sorts, because the petitioner seeks to encroach on that person's wealth or power. This is how typical patron-client relationships work, in which one donation is necessarily reciprocated by another one; some form of reciprocity is presumed. Various kinds of patron-client relationships are possible; for example, from the side of the client/petitioner—is the person petitioned a kinsman, a resident of his village, or even of the same *ethnos*? Is some duty of the petitioner implied in the petition? Some relationship expressed? Patron-client relationships are never altruistic but embody reciprocity of some sort. Hence, the petitioner necessarily gives the other

---

22. Eickleman (*The Middle East*, 181–87) distinguishes four types of names and their usage: (1) personal names; (2) nicknames; (3) names derived from occupation, origin, and affiliation; and (4) patrifiliative names, or names embodying one's parents and clan. As we saw earlier in the study of encomiastic "origins," honorable status depends upon geographical and generational identification. See also Pilch, *A Cultural Handbook to the Bible*, 88–93. I comment on the Matthean version of this story: "his enemies attempted to stigmatize him with many negative labels. In terms of origin, occupation, and affiliation, Jesus 'of Nazareth' who is the son of the carpenter carried negative honor status with some (John 1:46; 7:52)" (Neyrey, *Honor and Shame in the Gospel of Matthew*, 56–57).

23. If addressing Jesus is rare in Luke, equally infrequent is Jesus's addressing someone else by her or his name. One finds only that Peter/Simon is addressed by his name: "I tell you, Simon, the cock will not crow this day . . ." Although Luke's audience is told many names (Zechariah, Elizabeth, Joseph, and John, and so forth), only once is the mother of Jesus addressed by her name, and this by an angel sent by God: "Do not be afraid, Mary" (1:30). This reflects a cultural pattern that must be appreciated in terms of "honor."

person something, most likely honor and respect, thus putting the person petitioned under obligation to reciprocate somehow.

In regard to the patron, does he want this relationship? Will he allow himself to be taken advantage of? Does being a benefactor enhance the honor of the petitioned person? Is any type of reciprocity in view? Will the person petitioned act without any expectation of recompense? While members of a kinship group may ask parents for benefits (Luke 11:8–13), all other social interactions presume some form of reciprocity. So, a request can function as a challenge. Therefore, when leprous or blind petitioners cry out, "Jesus, Son of David, have mercy" (see, e.g., Luke 18:38), they at least proffer an honorific generational tag to Jesus's personal name ("Son of David"). So, they extend something with an expectation of some benefit in return. Are there expectations here?

The address in 4:34 contains a geographical tag ("of Nazareth"), not a generational tag ("son of David"). And so, two issues are front and center: addressing Jesus by his personal name and noting his birthplace: "*of Nazareth.*" Addressing someone by his personal name is itself a claim to advantage. But the addition of the tag "*of Nazareth*" is a social slight, a dishonor, simply because Nazareth is a mean birthplace. Luke and his audience understand that this mention of Jesus's origins does not honor him. As honorific as "Son of David" is, so abusive is "of Nazareth." Score one for the demon. So, the dishonoring of Jesus is expressed both in the demon's addressing him by his personal name and by the demon's mention of his birthplace.

The demon then changes weapons, from aggressive questions to a boast of his own power. "I know who you are, the Holy One of God" (4:34). The demon's attack proceeds in two ways. First, he claims to know Jesus: "I know who you are." Because Jesus and the demon are mortal enemies, this claim has nothing neutral in it and must be seen as a challenge that claims some advantage for the demon over Jesus. But where is the poison here? The remark "I know you," while not unfamiliar to Gospel readers, needs to be interpreted in terms of its cultural usage. This is not knowledge-as-information but implies some sort of knowledge-as-social-superiority. For example, Luke narrates that people address a householder as "Lord, Lord"—as their patron?—and by granting him this respect, claim a relationship with reciprocal benefits for themselves. By claiming to be loyal clients, they expect some reciprocity. In saying, "We ate and drank in your presence" (13:26), they claim to be regular clients, to whom the patron must reciprocate. Yet he, for his part, shames them when he says, "I *do not know* you" (13:25).[24]

Were he to know them, he would be acknowledging a relationship with duties to them, to their advantage. Knowing and not knowing imply relationships that express superior and inferior ranks, and thus duties to be paid, which is what justice means. But where does this superiority come from? If God, the source of all authority and power, acknowledges that Jesus is "my Son, the Beloved, with whom I am well pleased," whence comes the authority and power of the demon? He is issuing a vain claim; he speaks a lie. In short, he is boasting, making a dishonorable claim in this context.

Second, as correct as the address "the Holy One of God" might sound, it is a baited trap. Were it sincere, it would be a grant of significant honor to Jesus, but it would also mean that the demon is in fact subject to his enemy. Moreover, if the demon spoke truly, then Jesus would owe something to the demon; that is, that the demon would have some claim on him. How foolish to think that honor from an enemy is without peril! How foolish for a wise man such as Jesus not to perceive the sarcasm and treachery in a baited complement! This compares with the deceptive poison found in a later address to Jesus: "We know that you speak and teach rightly, and show no partiality, but truly speak the way of God . . ." (20:21). Thus, the demon seemingly shows respect, but only as a gambit, a ploy in a contest. The demon concedes something to gain something. By wisely discerning the deception and poison here, Jesus confirms his reputation for wisdom.

As with all chreiai, this one ends with a successful riposte by the one challenged, as Jesus subjects his challenger to his own authority and vanquishes him. If Jesus was shouted at when the challenge began, Jesus's first "rebuke" is a command, "Be silent!" If the demon sought any power

---

24. Although patron-client relations are now recognized in New Testament scholarship, less so is the social phenomenon of "reciprocity." One may enter the conversation with Gouldner, "The Norm of Reciprocity"; and the broad study of Gill et al., eds., *Reciprocity in Ancient Greece*; and van Wees, "Reciprocity in Anthropological Theory." Useful are specific studies such as Dolan, "Reciprocities in Homer"; and Dolan, "The Unequal Exchange between Glaucus and Diomedes." For scholars of the Hebrew Bible, see Stansell, "The Gift in Ancient Israel"; for New Testament scholars, see Malina, *Christian Origins and Cultural Anthropology*, 98–106. More recently, see Neyrey, "Lost in Translation."

Bultmann, "*gignōskō*," interpreted this passage in terms of denial of public recognition of someone, that is, honor. I understand this usage as "not lack of accurate knowledge, but rather a withholding of a grant of respect," that is, public recognition of someone (Neyrey, *Honor and Shame in the Gospel of Matthew*, 225). See Picirelli, "The Meaning of *Epignosis*."

or advantage over Jesus, he is totally repulsed: "Come out of him" (4:35). Thus, the demon yields his spoils and leaves the field empty-handed and overpowered (cf. Luke 11:17–22). An episode such as this is often labeled an exorcism, but it is better understood as a rhetorical chreia, which ceremonially confirms the role and status of the protagonist. Moreover, this chreia occurs in a synagogue meeting, and Luke would have us understand such a chreia to be a common element in that service. In this ritualized combat, moreover, Jesus is ceremonially confirmed as worthy of public voice: "'What kind of utterance is this? For with authority and power he commands the unclean spirits, and out they come!' And a report about him began to reach every place in the region" (4:36–37).

Summary and Conclusions

The use of modern anthropology to describe rituals and ceremonies yields significant benefits, which are not easily or convincingly found by other modes of reading. The modern jargon used to plot their typical choreography describes features that were practiced by ancient authors although not clearly described. Fresh insights into the narrative dynamics of a document are made evident, which simply cannot be achieved in any other way. There is, then, great benefit for a modern reader to use contemporary models of ritual and ceremony to understand Luke and Acts. From this chapter, we draw certain conclusions.

1. If status-elevation rituals advance the role and status of Jesus, ceremonies serve to confirm them.

2. Roles and status may be confirmed when a person successfully acts according to the popular expectations of one so designated. Ceremonial confirmations may be narrated as regular celebrations of Passover or as customary attendance in the synagogue.

3. Roles and statuses may also be confirmed by ritual combat, that is, by ceremonial testing of the ascribed role and status of the hero whose story is narrated.

4. In this regard, then, the genre chreia is shown to consist of a ceremony of ritualized conflict. Because chreia was a common genre used in the Gospels to narrate Jesus's actions, its contents and purpose would be immediately appreciated. May one suggest that if there is conflict in a

Gospel episode, the rhetorical genre most likely to be used to narrate it will be a chreia.

5. Moreover, this ritual combat may occur in a typical ceremonial service in a synagogue. For, as noted, synagogues are regularly portrayed as arenas of dispute and argument, as well as loci of judgment and chastisement.

6. Since our focus remains on how Luke establishes Jesus's role and status to have public speech, at least the ceremonies narrated in 4:1–38 and (as we will see next in the Appendix to this chapter) 6:1–11 serve to confirm the elevated status awarded Jesus in 3:21–22.

∽

APPENDIX

Chreia, Ritual Conflict, and Luke 6

Modern scholars never have enough examples of something or enough data to seal an argument. This being so, the following episodes in Luke 6 are offered as further example of the argument that many chreiai describe a ceremony of ritual conflict.

Ceremonial Conflict in the Grainfield (Luke 6:1–5)

The scene occurs, not in the typical locus of conflict, the synagogue, but in neutral territory, a grainfield. The timing, however, is the same, "the Sabbath." Jesus's disciples appear to be gleaning grain along the perimeter of a field, rubbing off the chaff, and eating the grain, presumably because they are hungry. It is lengthily stated in two catalogues of the Ten Words that rest on the Sabbath is mandated (Exod 20:8–11; Deut 5:12–15). This broad injunction, however, was constantly being interpreted, often in broader terms. Should the hungry work to eat on the Sabbath? May a man "untie his ox or his donkey from the manger, and lead it away to give it water" on the

Sabbath (13:15)? May a man on the Sabbath draw out his sheep from the pit into which it has fallen (Matt 12:11–12)? Pharisees, known as rule makers and enforcers, challenge expansions such as these. The disciples act with Jesus's approval, which is his claim to honor. Pharisees challenge it, with a question, of course: "Why are you doing what is not lawful on the sabbath?" (6:2). As expected, Jesus delivers the riposte in the form of a counterquestion: "Have you not read what David did when he and his companions were hungry?" (6:3–4). In fact, David ate loaves "which it is not lawful for any but the priests to eat" (6:4). The presumption in this exchange is typical of a chreia; the person challenged responds to the challenging question and silences the antagonist.

Thus, whether in a synagogue or grainfield, conflict is ritually narrated in terms of a chreia. Since the form and purpose of a chreia is to praise the successful defense of the protagonist's status, it operates as ceremonies do. But here, defense of status is not enough, for Jesus makes a significantly bolder claim to role and status: "The Son of Man is lord of the sabbath" (6:5).

Still More Ceremonial Conflict in a Synagogue (Luke 6:6–11)

In a subsequent synagogue appearance by Jesus Luke skips mention of any events in the meeting in order to focus only on the conflict that occurs. Jesus exercises his role and status, which deserve respect and honor: "He entered the synagogue and taught" (6:6). Thus, as in all chreiai, the protagonist appears as an honorable person, sufficiently prominent to provoke envy. The antagonistic judges are in place: "The scribes and the Pharisees watched him to see whether he would cure on the sabbath, so that they might find an accusation against him" (6:7). Their critical watching of Jesus serves here as the rhetorical equivalent of a challenging question. The protagonist, Jesus, who displays prowess because "he knew what they were thinking"(6:8) meets this challenge with a stinging riposte of both word and deed.

Everybody in the synagogue could see the man with a withered hand, the general crowd, as well as the antagonists, the scribes and Pharisees, and the protagonist, Jesus. In response to the challenge, Jesus summons the man with a withered hand to center stage so that all eyes and ears are focused. Jesus then asks a very hostile question, typical of a riposte: "Is it lawful on the sabbath to do good or to do harm, to save life or to destroy it?" (6:9). From the dynamics of the genre chreia we conclude that the rhetorical question asked expresses the antagonists' point of attack, and it is a deadly question for which there is no easy answer. Clearly, hostile and challenging judges are judging, and the protagonist is given no quarter—which is the typical choreography of a chreia. Although no particular name of Jesus is attacked, the critical scrutiny of him looks to his holiness, that is, his obedience to the Sabbath law, which was just contested in 6:1–5. The stakes here could not be higher. Obviously Jesus is the one designated by God (see 4:18–21) to perform beneficial actions, that is, "to do good . . . to save life." Jesus confirms this role and status by what he says and does: "'Stretch out your hand' . . . and his hand was restored" (6:10). According to the way a chreia works, Jesus has successfully defended his honor claim, because of which his enemies are scattered. Chreiai-as-conflicts, however, do not cease, as the enemy only withdraws to attack again: his judges "were filled with fury and discussed with one another what they might do to Jesus" (6:11).

PART 2

Reading Luke with Rhetorical Lenses

CHAPTER 5

How Beginnings Begin

THE TASK CONTINUES. We continue to argue that in chapters 1–4 Luke establishes the ethos of Jesus so that Luke's audience, as well as the narrative characters in the story, will appreciate the grounds for Jesus having public voice. Now we consider how orations and stories themselves typically begin. An orator had to establish an ethos either for himself or for his designated subject to ensure credible communication with his audience. Likewise, a prose writer such as Luke (or Josephus or Suetonius or Plutarch or Nepos) must do the same for his narrative characters. But building an ethos was not something left to chance; on the contrary, orators and writers explicitly studied formal, conventional rhetorical ways for doing this. In the course of their rhetorical studies, they learned to create proper beginnings. This chapter examines these beginnings as treated in classical rhetoric to show that, in fact, these were highly conventional,[1] because regular ways for creating them were mandated. And so, orators and authors learned of what such beginnings consisted.

Before we start, we must determine what we are talking about, because in taking up this topic we are walking into a terminological spider web. The neutral word *beginning* has no consistency among biblical scholars; for as often as they might use *beginning*,[2] they are just as likely to use terms like

---

1. Cadbury, "Commentary on the Preface of Luke."
2. Guelich, "The Beginning of the Gospel."

*Eröffnung,*³ *Anfang,*⁴ *prologue,*⁵ *introduction,*⁶ or *preface.*⁷ The terms are used interchangeably and without precision, so it is difficult to be sure what is meant by any of them. They are all terms current in modern historical and literary criticism, not ancient rhetoric. It is doubtful that ancient rhetoricians would accept any of them as corresponding to what they spoke about, namely, *prooimion, exordium,* and *principium.* Thus, before we consider how beginnings began, we must give attention to some ancient rhetorical discussion of them.

Ancient rhetoricians understood a *prooimiom* to be the first part of a speech: "The necessary parts of a speech are statement of the case and proof. These divisions are appropriate to every speech, and at the most the parts are four in number: exordium (*prooimion*), statement, proof, epilogue" (Aristotle, *Rhet.* 3.13.4). The Greeks called this first part a *prooimium,* and

---

3. Arnold, "Eröffnungswendungen in grieschischen und lateinischen Schriften."

4. Pokorny, "Anfang des Evangeliums"; Boring, "Mark 1:1–15 and the Beginning of the Gospel."

5. Seitz, "Gospel Prologues"; Gibbs, "Mark 1,1–15, Matthew 1,1–4,16, Luke 1,1–4,30, John 1,1–15"; Ferneberg, *Der Markusprologue*; Matera, "The Prologue as the Interpretative Key to Mark's Gospel."

6. Keck, "The Introduction to Mark's Gospel."

7. There is comparable imprecision on how to label Luke 1:1–4. First of all, "preface" seems interchangeable with "prologue," without any discussion of an underlying Greek term or genre. Except for the search for comparable "prefaces" in Hellenistic historiography, no consideration is given to their roots in rhetoric. Except for Cadbury, there is no formal discussion of what this is and how it functions. When Cadbury examines "the form of the preface," he urges that it "should be considered in the light of contemporary Hellenistic literature ("Commentary on the Preface of Luke," 490); but his footnotes talk about "prefaces" apart from any formal consideration of rhetoric. He refers, however, to "prefaces" under other terms, such as *anakephalaiōsis* and *argumentum* or *proekthesis,* which indicates that he is in touch with rhetoric. This becomes clearer when he suggests paraphrases for a "preface," which come right out of Aristotle and other rhetoricians. Moreover, he interprets the last term, *proekthesis,* as "a synopsis or *argumentum* giving the principal subjects to be discussed" (491), on occasion reducing it to "a detached label, a table of contents, or a preface." One of the rare commentators on Luke 1:1–4, Richard J. Dillon formally contests the facile identification of it as a "so-called prologue," ultimately arguing, "By strict contemporary standards, 'preface' or 'proemium' is a more suitable term for Luke 1 1–4 than the one we hear more frequently, 'prologue.'" Now the term is given substance. Moreover, it had been argued earlier by J.-P. Audet that Luke 1–2 together be considered the beginning; he argues that these chapters were conceived by Luke in the manner of classical Hellenistic *prooimia* ("prefaces"), the functions of which were described in Aristotle's *Rhetorica* 3.14. These prefaces prepared the reader to understand the body of the work, since otherwise there was a danger of misunderstanding the author's purpose.

the Romans, an *exordium* or a *principium*. Cicero explains the purpose of an exordium as follows:

> An exordium is a passage which brings the mind of the auditor into a proper condition to receive the rest of the speech. This will be accomplished if he becomes well-disposed, attentive, and receptive . . . An introduction [*principium*] is an address which directly and in plain language makes the auditor well-disposed, receptive, and attentive. (*Inv.* 1.15.20)

We should, then, ask about the proper contents of an exordium; of what did it consist? Aristotle is quite clear about this:

> But in speeches and epic poems the exordia provide *a sample of the subject*, in order that the hearers may know beforehand *what it is about*, and that the mind may not be kept in suspense, for that which is undefined leads astray; so then he who puts the beginning [*archēn*], so to say, into the hearer's hand enables him, if he holds fast to it, to follow the story. (*Rhet.* 3.14.6; italics added)

Aristotle next describes the function of the *prooimion/exordium*, which is "to make clear what is the end or purpose of the speech" (*Rhet.* 3.14.6), comparing it to "what the tragic poets do in proposing the subject of their dramas, if not at the outset, like Euripides, at least somewhere in the prologue, like Socrates."

When Aristotle compares the rhetorical *prooimion* to the beginning of dramatic works, he provides an important clue to its content and purpose.

> The exordium [*prooimion*] is the beginning [*archē*] of a speech, as the *prologue* [*prologos*] in poetry and the *prelude* [*proaulion*] in flute-playing; for all these are *beginnings* [*archai*], and are paving the way for what follows. The *prelude* resembles the exordium of epideictic speeches; for as flute-players begin by playing whatever they can execute skillfully and *attach it to the key-note*, so also in epideictic speeches should be the composition of the exordium; the speaker should say at once whatever he likes, give the key-note and then attach it to the main subject. (*Rhet.* 3.14.1; italics added)

Therefore, to learn about how classical beginnings begin, we follow the discussions found in ancient rhetorical handbooks.

Ancient Oratory and Beginnings

As a survey of ancient speeches or historical writings quickly shows, orators and writers had specific rhetorical instructions for beginning their works. They must begin somewhere and somehow—this is self-evident. What needs clarification is how they were taught to begin, how they were constrained in saying what they had to say. That is, their successful communication depended greatly on how they conventionally began. Orators and writers in the Greco-Roman world did not enjoy the independence of modern authors to be fresh, bold, and arresting when they begin. For, the basis for classical rhetorical training consisted in learning to write by means of rhetorical handbooks, which served to school students in the conventional ways of beginning. While it was occasionally possible to begin in medias res, orators and writers generally began with a conventional beginning. We can find examples of and rules for constructing one in two rhetorical places: first, in the sequence of parts of a speech, of which the exordium is the first item, and then in the use of the conventional topics from an encomium expected to tell the beginnings of a person's life.

Exordium

In oratory, the first part of an oration or speech, the *prooimion/exordium*, was constructed according to conventions both taught to an author and familiar to an audience.[8] It was essential for successful communication that authors immediately present their own ethos to their own audiences. Who is speaking? What are his qualifications to speak? About what or whom does he speak? Why should anyone listen? The initial part of a speech, the

---

8. Lausberg (*Handbook of Literary Rhetoric*, 122–23) constructed a synoptic figure of the traditional parts of a speech, from which we have selected three classical rhetoricians for comparison.

Aristotle	Cicero	Quintilian
Rhet. 3.13	*Inv.* 1.14	*Inst. Orat.* 3.9.1
1. *prosimian*	1. *exordium*	1. *prooemium/exordium*
2. *prosthesis*	2. *narratio*	2. *narratio*
3. *pistis*	3. *divisio*	3. *probatio*
4. *epilogos*	4. *confirmatio*	4. *refutatio*
5. *confutation*	5. *peroratio*	5. *peroratio*

exordium, was the obvious place to answer these questions and to present an acceptable ethos; and orators and prose writers knew the proper conventions for such a beginning. They were instructed to begin their exordia saying specific things about themselves, even as audiences came to expect the same. Cicero stated that an exordium is the proper place for an orator to present himself to his audience by establishing three things: (1) that he is well-informed about the topic, (2) that he conducts himself honestly and honorably, and (3) that he acts for the benefit of the audience, whether he tells them good news or bad (*Inv* 1.19–20). Beginnings were never left to chance but were constructed in conventional terms according to recognizable rhetorical forms.

Encomium

Rhetorical beginnings, however, should be constructed according to the topics listed in a conventional encomium. These topics, salient as far back as Aristotle, in time became the typical topics of the encomium genre found in Greco-Roman rhetoric. In it, orators or writers examined the life of a person to find honor in terms of conventional topics, such as a person's origins and nurture and training. The contents of each topic, moreover, were predictably standard, because the contents were found by means of conventional rules of discovery and composition. Furthermore, the topics in an enconium were deemed sufficient to present a person adequately in Greco-Roman culture.[9] Obviously, they constitute the beginning simply because they tell of the beginning of the life of the person being considered for praise.

One need only consult the comprehensive work of Richard A. Burridge on *bioi* to discover how common were these encomiastic topics.[10] The categories Burridge identifies have to do with birth, early years, and education. Burridge, however, being innocent of rhetoric, does not consider either a rhetorical exordium or a progymnastic encomium as the genre where these data are generally found. However, contemporary New Testament scholarship is coming to know the rhetorical handbooks called the progymnasmata, in which orators and writers were taught the proper

---

9. This was discussed earlier in chapter 3, in the exposition about a group-oriented person.

10. Burridge, *What Are the Gospels?*, 124–84.

genres for describing a person's life.[11] Much significant scholarship has happened since Burridge's study.

For this study, the most profitable line of inquiry is to consider encomiastic topics in order to learn what they taught as a proper beginning to an encomium. After this, we will examine how Mark, Matthew, and John begin their stories about Jesus, with special attention to how they employ the encomiastic topics of origins and nurture and training. What we find there will guide and support our consideration of Luke 1–4 in terms of the same topics.

We argue that the canonical Gospel writers began with recognizable rhetorical beginnings by narrating their traditional materials according to the rules for discoursing on origins and nurture and training. Their beginnings, then, were not left to chance, nor were the authors merely handing on early traditions. Nor were their interests predominately historical. They composed formal rhetorical beginnings according to conventional rules that would be readily recognized by their audiences. Such beginnings reflect the rhetorical purpose of establishing an ethos for the person whose story is being told. We argue further that the proper use of rhetoric was essential for this communication. The narrative could not be told in any other way.

Because these topics are significant for the argument in this chapter, we do well to reprise what was said about them earlier. First, *origins* means both geographical and generational origins. As regards geographical origins, it matters if a character is born in Nazareth (John 1:46) or Bethlehem (Matt 2:6); Paul was born in Tarsus, a no low-status city (Acts 21:39). As regards generational origins, since offspring are expected to be as noble as their parents and ancestors, it matters into which tribe they are born (so, for Jesus, that Joseph is a "son of David" [Luke 1:20]), or whether they enjoy a genealogy (see Luke 3:23–38). It matters if a parent is "righteous" or "holy." Significant also were the events accompanying a birth (such as a comet passing over Rome, or a star appearing in the east [Matt 2:1–12]), which were thought to indicate its importance. The importance of earthly births was heralded by heavenly messages, such as prophecies articulating the meaning of this birth. After origins, writers considered how this person was reared, what training, what nurture, what education did he have? These topics were the conventional ways for ancient orators and writers to introduce themselves or their characters, and they will serve us in the

---

11. Parsons and Martin, *Ancient Rhetoric and the New Testament*, 175–230.

same way. We will next examine how each evangelist introduces Jesus in encomiastic topics as a person deserving of public voice, whose teaching should be heard.

Mark

Mark's Gospel contains nothing about Jesus's geographical or generational origins, nor anything about his birth.[12] Mark moves immediately to what we call nurture and training—not that of Jesus, but that of John, who will speak about Jesus (i.e., the **Channel** of the **Sender**). Perhaps Mark presumes his audience knows something about John; but he says nothing about John's origins, birth, or training. Mark presents John as a person with an established public role to preach and teach, whose authority to do so Mark secures with a citation from Isa 40:3. This identifies John as a heavenly-sent "messenger," whose role it was to "prepare the way" (1:2, 3). According to Mark, John exercises this role by communicating two **messages**: first, by preaching "a baptism of repentance for the forgiveness of sins" (1:4–6) and then by announcing a word about Jesus's superior status (1:7–8). The first part of John's role included teaching about repentance and ritual washing, while in the second part John declares that a superior person is about to arrive, whose status vastly outranks that of John, namely, someone who is "mightier than I, the thong of whose sandal I am not worth to stoop down and untie" (1:7). After this, Mark immediately narrates that "Jesus came from Nazareth of Galilee and was baptized by John in the Jordan" (1:9). Thus, Mark begins his narrative by establishing the ethos of John to speak with authority.

Moreover, Mark continues his beginning by promptly stating that Jesus was formally invested with a superior role and status—and by God, no less:

> just as he was coming up out of the water, he saw the heavens torn apart and the Spirit descending like a dove on him. And a voice came from heaven, "You are my Son, the Beloved; with you I am well pleased." (1:10–11)

Without appreciating the rhetorical topics of origin, birth, and training, we might not see how Mark is concerned about the item of nurture and

---

12. The best treatment of the "beginning" of Mark remains that of Boring, "Mark 1:1–15 and the Beginning of the Gospel."

training. But, indeed, Mark is. He tells us that Jesus went to John, who was primarily a preacher/teacher. By this, Mark implies that Jesus went to John for some conventional purpose, which tradition identifies in Matthew as teaching about the imminent "kingdom of God" (Matt 3:2) or in Luke, about "the forgiveness of sins" (Luke 3:3). Why did Jesus go out into the desert, but to hear what some prophet had to say? Hence, John taught, to whose preaching Jesus listened, and so Jesus was in some way trained by John. This education climaxed with God's appearance, when the **Sender** himself spoke directly to Jesus, the **recipient**, a **message** that immediately established Jesus's role and status ("my Son, the Beloved; with you I am well pleased"). It is only afterwards that "Jesus comes to Galilee proclaiming the good news of God, and saying, "The time is fulfilled, and the kingdom of God has come near; repent, and believe in the good news" (1:14–15). Mark, therefore, begins with the rhetorical topic of nurture and training. He states that both John and God, by their training of Jesus, establish an ethos *for Jesus* at the beginning of the narrative.

Without a knowledge of rhetoric, we will quite likely fail to see in John's teaching a description of the nurture and training of Jesus. It is not enough just to put John in some historical trajectory of gospel traditions, for this does not account for reporting these data, much less presenting them according to the encomiastic topic of nurture and training. Mark's beginning, while brief, suffices to inform his audience of Jesus's worthiness to speak publicly on God's behalf about the kingdom of God.

Matthew

In contrast to Mark, Matthew begins with immediate interest in Jesus's origins, in a fulsome use of what encomiastic origins prescribed. First, Matthew informs his audience about Jesus's generational origins—that as a Son of David and a Son of Abraham, he enjoys an exceptionally worthy ancestry, a strong connection to the founding figures of the covenants of promise (1:1). Matthew builds on this dual generational remark about Jesus's origins by narrating a genealogy for Jesus, establishing his ancestral pedigree (1:2–17). The genealogy starts with a terse mention of Jesus's most significant ancestors (Abraham and David), the premier recipients of the covenants of promise, but repeats mention of them for their connection with other worthy ancestors.[13] This *past* has *present* significance,[14] and so Matthew expects his audience to appreciate that God's covenantal promises are now in the process of being realized. Whether through Jesus's genealogy or through a **message** about Jesus, the God of Israel stands out as the continuous **Sender** of data about Jesus in indirect speech.

The excellence of Jesus's parents, however, is initially clouded. Although Joseph, a son of David, is a "righteous" man (1:19), his betrothed is pregnant, but not by him. This tarnishes any honor he derives from his genealogy. Joseph may be "righteous," but Mary's pregnancy does not speak to her virtue. In their culture, her pregnancy by a man other than her betrothed is an insurmountable obstacle, so acute that Joseph contemplates breaking the betrothal. At least he would be acting honorably in this situation. Therefore, the **Sender** must send a clarifying **message** about the forthcoming child by means of a reliable **channel** to a worthy **recipient**, to resolve the crisis. The **Sender's** angel brings a **message** that testifies that Mary enjoys divine favor: "The child conceived in her is from the Holy Spirit" (1:20). The angel, moreover, announces a heavenly chosen name for the child, Jesus, which ascribes to him a noble role, "He will save his people from their sins" (1:21). And in this way Jesus's generational origins are defended and exalted; all obstacles are resolved for the **recipient**, Joseph.

As regards Jesus's geographical origins, Matthew presumes that his parents reside in Nazareth of Galilee. But Jesus was born in Bethlehem of Judea. This birthplace, as well as the claim that Jesus is himself "son of David" (1:1) and that his putative father is "Joseph, son of David" (1:20) may be a tradition passed on to Matthew and his audience, as well as the claim that Jesus was himself "son of David" (1:1). Matthew, however, takes pains to narrate that the proper geographical site for the birth of this royal heir must be David's royal city. These data are of such special significance for Jesus's geographical origins that Matthew informs his audience how Bethlehem should be evaluated according to Israel's Scriptures. Magi come from afar to honor "the one who has been born the king of the Jews" (2:2). Initially no one seems to know where a new king should be born.

---

13. For a history of scholarship on Matthew's genealogy, see Brown, *The Birth of the Messiah*, 65–95; on the social function of this genre, see Rohrbaugh, "The Social Function of Genealogies"; and Rohrbaugh, "Legitimating Sonship—A Test of Honour."

14. Its recitation, then, might be considered a "ceremony" that confirms the role and status of Jesus.

These wise men must consult other wise men ("chief priests and scribes") to learn the geographical birthplace of this new king (2:5).[15] Because they too have no firsthand information, they consult their own best source, the Scriptures of Israel, in particular, the prophet Micah. Accordingly, "Bethlehem" should be evaluated as the worthy place for the birth of Israel's king: "But you, O Bethlehem of Ephrathah, / who are one of the little clans of Judah, / from you shall come forth for me / one who is to rule in Israel" (Mic 5:2).[16] The force of the argument could not be stronger: "... for so it was written by the prophet" (Matt 2:5). Therefore, the **Sender**, the God of Israel, sends a **message**, both old and new, to **recipients** by means of the **channel**, Israel's Scriptures as they were interpreted by Jerusalem's elite. The **message** is about Jesus, who is not yet an actor in the drama. He is only spoken about.

In the rules for an encomium, rhetoricians were taught to search for extraordinary events accompanying the hero's birth. Matthew's remarks on this indicate a full understanding of this topic: (1) angels and dreams both inform and protect the narrative characters;[17] (2) a new star actually moves and so guides the *magoi*, and (3) "prophecies" from the Scriptures are noted as "fulfilled." First, an angel informs Joseph of God's workings (1:20-21), whereas dreams secure the escape of both the *magoi* and the family of Jesus (2:12-13), as well as their safe return (2:20, 22). Thus, the **Sender** continuously uses various modes (dreams, the star, prophecies) to communicate a **message** to a series of **recipients**. The **Sender**, who manages all events here, communicates *about* Jesus; and the **Sender** is the exclusive architect and guarantor of the narrative.

The star has received much attention, mostly from those concerned with astronomy and the star's historicity.[18] But rarely is it considered in terms of encomiastic origins, namely, as an extraordinary event which accompanies a significant birth.[19] While references to extraordinary events

---

15. See the extended discussion in Brown, *The Birth of the Messiah*, 165-201.

16. Although he does not consider Jesus's birth in Bethlehem in terms of geographical origins, Krister Stendahl ("*Quis et Unde?* An Analysis of Mt 1-2") has been very influential in scholarship; see Brown, *The Birth of the Messiah*, 184-85, 412-15, 421-23.

17. J. Hanson, "Dreams and Visions."

18. For the history of interpretation of the star, see Brown, *The Birth of the Messiah*, 610-13.

19. This is most notable in the study of the genres of a progymnasmata, such as that of Parsons and Martin, *Ancient Rhetoric and the New Testament*, 175-230.

are few in the extant progymnasmata,[20] the fact that so many prose writers of ancient times actually mention them attests that such materials were expected and readily understood. Finally, it was part of the ancient study of astronomy to correlate events on earth with heavenly phenomena, as has been shown in several recent studies of Revelation.[21] Unlike any other celestial phenomenon, this star rose in the east and went "ahead of them" "until it stopped over the place where the child was." (2:9). Its very movement is itself communication. Finally, "oracles," i.e. past prophecies in Israel's Scriptures, were regularly noted as being "fulfilled." These fulfilled prophecies speak to the **Sender's c**ontrol of events. They serve to impress Matthew's audience with the significance of the communication.

Therefore, although many examine the materials in Matt 1–2, few have recognized them in cultural and rhetorical terms. The data in Matt 1–2 are hardly miscellaneous items, like scraps of information found in various places and collected here. Whatever their location in the history of gospel traditions, they are very conventional topics that are readily requested in encomiastic origins. Their rhetorical significance lies in appreciating them as typical parts of a familiar rhetorical genre, constructed according to conventional rules, and crafted to proclaim the honorable ethos of Jesus.

As regards Jesus's nurture and training, Matthew follows gospel tradition when next he narrates that Jesus went out to John: "Jesus came from Galilee to the Jordan to John to be baptized by him" (3:13). But one does not just "go to John" for baptism; John, whose ethos is that of a prophet, taught and exhorted those who came to him, excoriating some (3:7–10) and affirming the righteousness of others (3:14–15). People who come to John traveled considerable distances, such as from "Jerusalem, all Judea and all the region about the Jordan" (3:5) and "from Galilee" (3:13). Therefore, we may presume from these remarks that they remained for some time, long enough to experience a liminal period of hearing John before "confessing their sins" and being baptized (3:6). We consider this period as a time of

---

20. Hermogenes says: "You will mention also any marvelous occurrences at birth, for example from dreams or signs or things like that" (*Preliminary Exercises*, 16, quoted in Kennedy, trans., *Progymnasmata*); and Menander Rhetor, "If any divine sign occurred at the time of his birth, either on land or in the heavens or on the sea, compare the circumstances of those of Romulus, Cyrus, and similar stories, since in these cases also there were miraculous happenings connected with their birth the dream of Cyrus' mother, the suckling of Romulus by the she-wolf" (*Treatise* 2.371.5–14, quoted in Russell and Wilson, eds. and trans., *Menander Rhetor*).

21. See Malina, *On the Genre and Message of Revelation*, 12–22; see also Malina, "Apocalyptic and Territoriality."

nurture and training, that is, a time when John's audience prepared for a purification quite different from that found in the Temple.

Like Mark, Matthew treats the relationship of John and Jesus as the occasion for the Jesus's own nurture and training. Again, John is authorized to speak because of a specific prophecy by Isaiah (3:2–3). And Matthew notes that John taught a program of baptism for the remission of sins (3:5–10), after which he describes Jesus according to a conventional syncrisis. Matthew attests to Jesus's higher status with three remarks by John about (1) "not [being] worthy to carry his sandals" (3:11), (2) the superiority of Jesus's actions—"he will baptize you with the Holy Spirit and fire" (3:11), and (3) Jesus's "consent" to allow John to wash him so as "to fulfil all righteousness" (3:15). John's role is primarily that of preacher—that is, he gives instruction on proper nurture and training to those who come to him.

Jesus, therefore, experienced some form of nurture and training from his mentor John. Inasmuch as John proclaimed, "Repent, for the kingdom of heaven is at hand" (3:2), the very repetition of this by Jesus, "Repent for the kingdom of heaven is at hand" (4:17) implies that Jesus learned at least this from his mentor. Thus, while the episode narrated in 3:1–15 may well be part of the tradition that Matthew received, it should also be interpreted in encomiastic terms as Jesus's nurture and training. The probability of this increases as one recognizes how Matthew properly followed encomiastic conventions for Jesus's origins and birth. Thus, Matthew begins his narrative with formal recognition of the encomiastic conventions appropriate for speaking about an honorable person. By virtue of this beginning, Matthew has established for Jesus a proper ethos so that he may legitimately "go about all Galilee, teaching in their synagogues and preaching the gospel of the kingdom" (Matt 4:32). According to Matthew, then, Jesus's ethos proved to be acceptable to synagogue audiences, as it was said, "His fame spread throughout all Syria . . . And great crowds followed him from Galilee, the Decapolis, Jerusalem, Judea, and from beyond the Jordan" (4:24–25).

John

Commentators label John 1:1–18 in very different ways. It surely is a beginning, since it begins the narrative. Some label it a "prologue,"[22] others a

---

22. See Harris, *Prologue and Gospel*, 14–16.

"proem,"[23] and still others a "preface."[24] For the purposes of this study, let us simply call it for now a beginning, similar to what other gospels and *bioi* have. Inasmuch as we have used the topics of the encomium to examine the data in those other beginnings, we should be consistent and use them here as well to understand the beginning in 1:1–18. In what sense do origins and nurture and training befit the Logos, the only Son of the Father, and Jesus Christ?

Geographical Origins

In the beginning, the Logos is said to have a *geographical* location, that of the heavenly, not earthly realm. The Logos, then, *has* a geographical location, which, however, is not on earth.[25] According to ancient Israelites, cosmic geography consisted of many layers, possibly four (Job 11:7–9), but generally only three: heaven, earth, and the sea (Phil 2:10; Rev 5:13). Moreover, as regards heavenly geography, the Most High God was enthroned high above the ordinary heavens. Thus, even heaven had a *geography*. The ancient cultural meanings of space and place do not at all correspond to those of modern readers, which is to say that they and we do not imagine the world in the same way.[26] We, of course, seek to understand how they considered geography, and so how they imagined that the Logos was *somewhere*.[27]

Generational Origins

As regards generational beginnings, nothing is clear in the beginning about the Logos until the end of the beginning (1:18), where the unique *Son* is located "close to the Father's heart." At this point, the author has finally

---

23. Dodd, *The Interpretation of the Fourth Gospel*, 292–96.

24. Robinson ("The Relation of the Prologue to the Gospel of St. John") states that "The *Prologue* is . . . like most *prefaces*, written after the work it *introduces*, drawing its themes together. It is a definite addition more like a *preface* to a second addition—setting the original work in a new context" (124–25, italics added).

25. What is needed is a scholarly investigation of what "place and space" mean in ancient literature, and in the Fourth Gospel in particular; see Neyrey, "Spaces and Places."

26. Neyrey, "Spaces and Places," 64–74.

27. Prepositions such as *pros* often express location: *where* is the Logos? In some sense located *before* God. Moreover, *epi* in 1:18 also implies location.

expressed a relationship between the two figures in generational terms, as Son and Father. Granted that this relationship is only slowly revealed, it invites readers to return to the initial mention of the Logos as *pros ton theon* (1:1, 2). Although there seems to be nothing generational here, a relationship is nevertheless expressed. Just as the Logos ("the true light") is said to have a change of geographical location ("coming into the world"), so too the Logos reveals more of his relationship *pros ton theon*, now in generational terms: he is said to have "glory as of the *only Son of the Father*" (1:14, RSV). Thus, some assertion of generational relationship is being made. So, at the end of the beginning, this figure, who is "the only Son of God," can explain his father. In a culture of group-oriented persons, a son should be like his father; this is what is implied by the insistence that a male person can be adequately known as the son of this or that person.

One way of testing the previous argument is to examine controversies about geographical and generational origins in the course of John's Gospel. Geography in the Fourth Gospel proves to be a constant and controversial issue. Previously I identified many different categories that the author used for classifying place in the gospel, all taken from the narrative itself.[28] Because those categories aid in understanding the topic of geographical origins, they have a place here. While all of them apply to Jesus, the only Son of God, they describe a figure in considerable motion.

1. Whence and whither: the classic reference is, "I know whence I have come and whither I am going, but you do not know when I come or whither I am going" (8:14 RSV; see also 7:27–28; 9:29–30; 16:5).

2. Descent and ascent: "Jesus, knowing that the Father had given all things into his hands, and that he had come from God and was going to God" (13:3; see also 6:62).[29]

3. From above and from below: "You are from below, I am from above; you are of this world, I am not of this world" (8:23).

4. Nazareth/Galilee and Bethlehem:[30] "Yet we know where this man is from; but when the Messiah comes, no one will know where he is

---

28. Neyrey, *The Gospel of John*, 46–47, 77–80, 144–49, 154–57, 235, 282–83.

29. Meeks, "The Man from Heaven"; Borgen, "The Son of Man Saying in John 3:13–14," 110–12.

30. Neyrey, *The Gospel of John*, 126, 144, 149.

from" (7:27); "the Messiah is descended from David and comes from Bethlehem, the village where David lived" (7:42).[31]

Yet only Jesus knows whence he came and whither he goes; all others do not, despite repeated claims. Moreover, what Jesus says about this is generally phrased in double-meaning words, and according to the Johannine figure, statement—misunderstanding—clarification. Only the enlightened audience knows what Jesus knows. But it is clear that the Fourth Gospel is much concerned with geography, both heavenly and earthly, which begins in the beginning.

As was the case with controversies over geography, so also we find comparable ones concerning the generational origins of Jesus, which is hardly a minor matter in John. Twice in John's Gospel the identity of Jesus's earthly father is referenced, but neither reference gives honor to Jesus (1:45; 6:42). When Philip finds Nathanael, he describes Jesus in perfect cultural terms, namely, in terms of geographical and generational origins, "Jesus son of Joseph from Nazareth" (1:45). Nathanael's dismissal, however, is quickly reversed when he acknowledges a new generational identity for Jesus, "You are the Son of God!" (1:49). Moreover, Jesus declares a new geography for himself when he tells the disciples that they will see "heaven opened and the angels of God ascending and descending upon the Son of Man" (1:51). Throughout John 6, Jesus talks about a Father, a heavenly one, from whom he has "come down." The hearers, however, challenge both the generational and geographical origins: "Is not this Jesus, the son of Joseph, whose father and mother we know?" (6:42). As with the matter of geography, knowledge about generation is opaque to this audience; they are not able to grasp spirit because they are flesh. Nevertheless, generational matters are prominent in John, an introduction to which is made in the beginning.

Nurture and Training

The term *Logos* implies that someone is speaking. Inasmuch as the Logos is *pros ton theon*, the Logos must somehow and in some way contain what *theos* was expressing. This Logos knows much, for immediately "all things were made through him." Elsewhere, Wisdom is credited with creation; moreover this metaphor implies that wisdom has both plan and power,

---

31. Meeks, "Galilee and Judea in the Fourth Gospel."

not of itself, but as given by God. Whence comes the Logos of the cosmos except from being *pros ton theon*? The Logos acts as taught, spoken to, or instructed. Indeed, "all things were made *through* him, so that the actor *theos* is acting *through* another. This Logos, we are told, has "life," which is "the light of all people" (1:4). Because of the contrast between light/Logos and darkness/world (1:5, 9), the Logos functions as a teacher himself: "he was the true light that enlightens every mortal; he was coming into the world" (my trans.). Teachers, as all know, were both unsuccessful and ultimately successful. The absence of success is not failure on the part of the teacher, but of the audience: "He was in the world . . . yet the world did not know him. He came to what was his own, and his own people did not accept him" (1:10–11). But some "received him," to whom "he gave power to become children of God" (1:12). Although generational origins for some are established (1:13), the success of the Logos as teacher came when "we [saw] his glory," not as Logos, but "glory as of *a father's only son*." A chip off the old block? Like Father, like Son? This figure may not need nurture and training himself, but he serves that function to others. Finally, it is stated that "No one has ever seen God" (1:18); true enough, but that does not mean "darkness" (1:4) or dullness (1:14). This figure is the unique source of knowledge about God, which is readily communicated: "the only Son, who is close to the Father's heart, has made him known" (1:18). Thus, nurture and training are of maximum importance here, not that of the Logos, only Son of God, but that of all who are coming into the light. Moreover, although some denigrate Jesus because he has no proper learning (7:15), he constantly speaks the "words of God."

These data argue that John is using the same topics from the encomium that were used in other Gospels. To be sure, they reflect the maverick perspective of that gospel; but as topics, they are operative categories in the beginning of the Fourth Gospel. Confirmation comes from following their treatment in the rest of the narrative. John's true audience, then, will not hear as does Nicodemus, hearing only "earthly things" (3:12)

Luke

Eventually we will make a synopsis of the beginnings of all four Gospels to see what data they contain and how that was presented. Before we can do this, however, we must examine Luke 1–4, his beginning.[32] The same rubric should be followed: that is, using the topics origins and nurture and training as templates for collecting and understanding data. As was the case with Matthew, it would appear that we have much data and that the encomiastic topics seem quite appropriate for understanding them.

Generational Origins

Luke begins with mention of Jesus's parents and relatives. The designated mother is a blood relative of Elizabeth, one of the daughters of Aaron, who is married to a priest of the division of Abijah (1:5). Mary herself is betrothed to Joseph, "of the house of David" (1:27). In the ancient world, one's tribe was generally a source of honor, and so it matters that Jesus is related both to priestly and kingly clans.

Later in the narrative, Luke records a genealogy for Jesus that ascribes for him the most prominent ancestors in the history of Israel. In the genealogy we learn that Jesus is acclaimed both as a descendent of the tribe of Judah, and as in descent from Israel's patriarchs, the founders of the house of Israel: ". . . son of Perez, son of Judah, son of Jacob, son of Isaac, son of Abraham" (3:33–34). But the descent from the illustrious ancestors continues even further back, " . . . son of Shem, son of Noah, son of Lamech, son of Methuselah . . . son of Seth, the son of Adam, son of God" (3:36–38).

Geographical Origins

Geography reinforces generation, because Joseph, of the house of David, must travel "from the town of Nazareth in Galilee to Judea, to the city of David called Bethlehem, because he was descended from the house [*oikos*] and family [*patria*] of David" (2:4). So, the most recent descendent of David will be born in David's royal city. This information is made known by heavenly messengers to shepherds in the region: "To you is born this day in the city of David a Savior, who is the Messiah, the Lord" (2:11).

Although Jerusalem's shrine is not a geographical origin for Jesus, it is the place where immediately after his birth, the following ritual events

---

32. For a fulsome presentation of this material, see Neyrey, *An Encomium for Jesus*, 18–49.

in the life of this new son of David occur. Jerusalem's temple was necessarily the appropriate location for the dedication of this firstborn to God: "They brought him up to Jerusalem to present him to the Lord" (2:22), for this is where they must come to offer a sacrifice (2:24). Moreover, two prophets are there at the same time, who announce the significance of the newborn to all in the temple. Jerusalem was the place to which the family of Jesus made annual pilgrimage for Passover, "Now every year his parents went to Jerusalem for the festival of the Passover" (2:41), as well as the site where Jesus had rabbinic conversation for three days (2:46). Nazareth may be the residence of Jesus's parents, the place to which they returned after ceremonies in Jerusalem, but it makes a formidable contrast to the true place where the "Son of David" would come.

Accompanying Events

What heavenly angels are to the narrative in Matthew, prophetic figures are in Luke. On the topic of origins, encomiastic authors focused on special, even heavenly, signs to articulate the importance of this birth. In Luke, two prophets, Simeon and Anna, fill this role. Simeon is introduced to Luke's audience as "righteous and devout" (2:25); indeed "the Holy Spirit was upon him." Already it had been prophesied to him that he would live long enough to see the "Lord's Christ" (2:26) This prophet, already groomed and ready, was led by the Spirit to the temple, where he took the child in his arms. And, holding the child, Simeon "praised God," and proclaimed that he was seeing "your salvation" in the person of the child (2:28, 30). Balancing Simeon, the prophetess Anna, herself of considerable pedigree ("the daughter of Phanuel, of the tribe of Asher" [2:36]) is already prepared for her task: "She never left the temple but worshiped there with fasting and prayer night and day" (2:37). She too confesses God and speaks of the child to "all who were looking for the redemption of Jerusalem" (2:38). Two prophets, then, speak of the Lord's anointed to all who would listen to them.

Therefore, as regards encomiastic origins, all of the rules taught in the rhetorical handbooks are followed in Luke 1–2. Considerable data about Jesus's origins are gathered and apportioned according to the template of an encomium. Luke, the author, knows the genre and its conventional topics, and so too does the audience to whom Luke writes.

Nurture and Training

The path forward is hindered by several stumbling blocks. Luke narrates in 4:16–20 that Jesus stood up, opened the book, and found the place and read it. Moreover, Luke reports that Jesus attended symposia and participated as was culturally appropriate. But it is inconceivable that Jesus received any literary training, even if only to read. That level of education was simply out of reach for a peasant artisan, because of either cost or lack of opportunity or lack of social status. Luke, it would seem, has promoted Jesus from a peasant village to a more urban setting and gives him comparable status advantages.

Yet Luke is also at pains to inform his audience that Jesus was properly socialized, not made literate, but made fit in his cultural world to know his place and keep it. The place to find this displayed is in the post-Passover episode where Jesus intentionally separates himself from his parents and converses in the temple with "the teachers" (2:46). Luke and his audience know for certain that while Jesus performs well in question-and-answer games with Israel's "teachers," he lacks a more fundamental and significant training in obedience to his parents. It has been argued, moreover, that Jesus's skill in debate is itself a convention, namely, that the hero was portrayed as precocious in learning as a youth. If modern readers consider what was the appropriate nurture and training for a twelve-year-old, they would look again at what Duncan J. M. Derrett said about this. Jesus was indeed "socialized" to fit into his cultural world. For a peasant artisan, this would have little to do with a teacher-pupil relationship. Rather, we should ask what a mature person would look like in Jesus's cultural world. The issue, then, is not information or academic education, but what values and virtues Jesus must learn so as to live up to that the expectations of his family and peers. Derrett summarizes what proper socialization here would mean:

> A list of what we might call "gentlemanly" qualities as the educated Hebrew understood them would be very short. "Good conduct," "deportment" was conveyed by the characteristic phrase *derek erets*, not quite "the way of the world" . . . but rather "conformity with the ideal norm, behaving oneself with propriety"—a complacent concept offering no challenge: good manners rather than good morals.[33]

---

33. Derrett, *Jesus' Audience*, 67.

We might express this as "Honor your father and your mother" or as "He learned obedience." Derrett remarked further: "After a child reached the age of 5, he began to learn that his society was duty-oriented, not right-oriented . . . no one [society] was concerned about his rights; everyone wanted to know his duties and wished to be thought 'worthy to fulfil them.'"[34]

To be sure, Jesus at twelve years old was by no means trained in the ways expected of him. By the time Jesus was about thirty years old he would have presumably reached the completion of his nurture and training. But for the time being, Luke compresses all that is needed to know about the boy into the remark: "Then he went down with them and came to Nazareth, and was obedient to them . . . and Jesus increased in wisdom and in years" (2:51–52).

Luke crafts a beginning in the same way we have seen in Matthew. When we process the narrative in Luke 1–2, we can see that Luke employs the traditional topics of an encomium to begin his narrative. It was there that a detailed inquiry was made into Luke's use of the particular topics of origins and nurture and training. But since the focus here is on beginnings, some repetition of the outlines of that previous inquiry are suitable here, if only for the purpose of comparison. Two questions should be asked: first, did Luke follow the encomiastic topics of origins and nurture and training? Yes, so it has been shown. Second, how does Luke's beginning compare with those of other gospels? It would seem that he is both shaping many traditional data about Jesus in a recognizable rhetorical form, and that his rhetorical effort is identical with that of Matthew and comparable to how other Gospels begin. We pass over here the differences between Luke and other Gospel writers, because we are focusing only on the rhetorical genre that Luke and others are using.

How, then, do gospel authors begin their narratives? Granted they have access to many pieces of traditional data, how did they arrange them? What rhetorical form or genre did they following in presenting their data in conventional ways that their audiences would recognize?

---

34. Derrett, "An Apt Student's Matriculation," 105.

Encomium	Mark	Matthew	John	Luke	Paul
Origins					
Geographical	------	Bethlehem, in Judah	heavenly, then earthly	Bethlehem	Tarsus, a no low-status city
Generational	-------	Son of Abraham, son of David Genealogy	only son of the Father	Mary, blood relative of priestly clan; Joseph, son of David	"a member of the people of Israel, of the tribe of Benjamin, a Hebrew born of Hebrews" (Phil 3:5)
heavenly portents and signs	-------	star, dreams, prophecies	John witnessing	angelic messengers, prophets interpreting	------
Nurture and Training	tutored by John	tutored by John	*Logos pros theon*	"He was obedient to them"; "He increased in wisdom and in years" (Luke 2:51–52)	"brought up in this city at the feet of Gamaliel, educated strictly according to our ancestral law" (Acts 22:3)

Summary and Conclusions

The preceding study of Gospel beginnings answers one question. Were the Gospel writers concerned to establish a recognizable foundation for Jesus to have public voice? Indeed, they were. Moreover, at least Matthew, John, and Luke (and Paul) knew of the appropriate topics where their data should be gathered. Moreover, their use of encomiastic materials establishes Jesus's role and status for his public voice. He is, to be sure, no bumpkin from a backwater village (cf. Acts 4:13), but a person of ancestry and pedigree, who is assuredly worthy of public voice. The clarity with which the Gospel writers employ these encomiastic topics speaks also to the expectations of their audiences, for such was the custom in oratory and writing to present a person in this way. It matters, moreover, that the rhetorical genres for establishing Jesus's right to public voice were commonly taught in rhetoric in general and in the rhetorical handbooks called the progymnasmata. Thus, materials contained in them were familiar to author and audience alike. What, then, do we know when we know all of this?

1. When modern readers of the four Gospels put these beginnings in some comparative form, they clearly see that the evangelists were concerned about how their narratives about Jesus should begin. Matthew, John, and Luke are quite conscious about beginning their narratives with a proper beginning.

2. In Matthew, John, and Luke, moreover, those proper beginnings feature conventional materials accurately identified as topics from encomiastic concerns for origins, namely geographical and generational data. Furthermore, this is by no means esoteric information. It may seem strange to modern readers, but it was commonly expected of authors trained in rhetoric and appreciated by their audiences

3. Modern readers familiar with classical rhetoric can quickly identify the individual parts of this *genre* of encomium, as well as the specific topics in them, such as origins and nurture and training. They would also know the contents of the topic of origins—that it includes geographical and generational data. And so, rhetorically literate readers can begin to read Luke as he expected ancient listeners would hear his narrative—that is, according to the genre and topics of an encomium.

4. The proper way for ancient orators and writers to communicate these data was by means of rhetoric, that is, according to the rhetorical genres developed in that ancient world. Individual items about origins might appear incidentally, but to communicate the honorable quality of a person's pedigree, the *genre* of encomium (or at least its conventional topics) would have to be used. Inasmuch as orators and writers sought to communicate, they invariably chose forms or genres that their audiences were able to understand. In the literature of the ancient world, this meant that they used the rhetorical modes of expression taught them as the apt means of communication.

5. When modern readers of Luke know the rhetorical contents of an encomium, they also know that after attention is given to a person's origins, the audience can expect an ancient author to show concern

for that person's proper nurture and training. Of course, this implies some chronological perspective of a person's development, but it is also rhetorically formalized with proper content in the predictable topics of the encomium. These observations are not in opposition, but collaborate in creating a proper ethos.

CHAPTER 6

Making a Rhetorical Ethos for Jesus

Investigating Luke 1–4, we should be aware that Luke makes an ethos both for himself (1:1–4) and for Jesus (1:5—4:37). In a subsequent chapter, we will consider how and why Luke must make an ethos for himself, but here we concentrate on how Luke goes about establishing an ethos for Jesus. Once more, because readers may not be familiar with this rhetorical material, it seems good to describe it first so that all might be thinking the same about an ancient rhetorical item.

What Is Meant by an Ethos?

The rhetorical term ethos has come up in most of the earlier chapters of this book, but only in passing. When considering Luke 1–4 in terms of communication modeling, we noted that the purpose of the **Sender** in sending **message** after **message** was to build up the character of Jesus, climaxing in 3:21–22. As we saw, all of the **Sender's messages** have to do with establishing a foundation for the character of Jesus in order for him to enjoy public voice. Luke began this in the beginning of his narrative, as the first words about Jesus were spoken. At stake was his role and status, which was articulated by authorized **channels**. This progressive construction of his character by remarks from angels and prophets all serve to build for Jesus a proper ethos, the essential qualification for him to speak in public. It is time now to discuss what a proper ethos is; that is, what constitutes one, and where it belongs in an oration or in prose writing?

Were we writing a history of rhetoric, we would necessarily begin with Aristotle and his discussion of it in his *Rhetorica*. Jakob Wisse wrote this history for us more than thirty years ago, tracing the development of it from Aristotle, through the period between Aristotle and Cicero, and through Cicero's *De Oratore*.[1] And, indeed, a closer consideration of this formal rhetorical material will be made in the next chapter. But here we look to rhetorical materials closer to the time of Luke—indeed, materials that seem to have formed an important part of Luke's own rhetorical training, namely, the rhetorical handbooks known as the progymnasmata.

Encomium and Ethos

Why return to the genre encomium? What claim does it make to provide information essential to the formation of an ethos? Before Aristotle, when orators presented the person whom they wished to praise, they talked casually about the very topics that in time became the formal topics of the genre encomium.[2] Aristotle himself describes "the characters [ēthē] of men according to their emotions, habits, ages and fortunes . . . By fortune I mean noble birth, wealth, power and their contraries" (*Rhet.* 2.12.2). He goes on to describe characteristics of noble birth: "The idea of noble birth refers to excellence of race, that of noble character not degenerating from the family type . . . For in the generations of men there is a crop as in the fruits of the field sometimes, if the race is good, men born out the common are born in it" (*Rhet.* 2.15.1–3). We noted earlier the contribution of Richard Burridge, who identified certain "internal features" of ancient *bioi* that correspond to what will be identified as topics of the progymnastic genre of the encomium. His remarks are important for our return to the encomium, and so we quote him:

> A number of standard, typical biographical topics or motifs recur throughout these works [early Greco-Roman *bioi*]. Nepos conveniently lists some at the start of *Epamonidas*: "We shall talk first about his ancestry, next his education and his teachers, then about his habits and traits of character and anything else which is worth remembering; then finally about his deeds, which many place before the virtues of his mind" (*De viris illustribus XV: Epam.* 1.4). Some of these occur in all or most of our works.[3]

---

1. Wisse, *Ethos and Pathos from Aristotle to Cicero*.
2. They are regularly mentioned in the funeral oration delivered either at the burial of a warrior or on the anniversary of his death; on the use of funeral orations as sources of epideictic rhetoric, see Neyrey, "The 'Noble Shepherd' in John 10."
3. Burridge, *What Are the Gospels?*, 141.

Although not attending to the genre of encomium as found in a progymnastic encomium, Burridge nevertheless identified the topics appropriately: (1) ancestry, (2) birth, (3) boyhood and education, (4) great deeds, (5) virtues, and (6) death and consequences.[4] Important for us is the digest of these topics by an encomiastic author himself.

At this point, we can appreciate why, in the first chapter, much time spent on showing how Luke's narrative about Jesus conforms to the conventional topics of the genre encomium. The benefits of that study can be mentioned quickly as illustrative of Luke's formation of an ethos for Jesus.

A proper ethos should feature mention of a person's origins, geographical and generational. It was not incidental, then, that Luke narrated Jesus was *not* born in Nazareth, a village of mean reputation (John 1:46), but in Bethlehem, "the city of David" (2:11). In regard to generational origins, Joseph belongs to the house of David, the tribe of Judah, Israel's most celebrated clan. In Luke's genealogy, he traces Jesus's ancestry back through kings (especially David and his line) and through patriarchs (especially Abraham) back to Adam, son of God. Moreover, celestial phenomena accompany Jesus's birth, indicating that the heavenly world greatly honors the child born on earth. We conclude that by narrating the origins of Jesus according to the encomiastic topic of origins, Luke establishes the foundations of a noble and worthy ethos for Jesus to eventually become a mature public speaker.

Building on this foundation, Luke tells his audience about the nurture and training of Jesus, indicating both Jesus's precociousness and his proper upbringing in the essential kinship virtue of obedience to his parents. Before Jesus can manifest his complete faithfulness to God, he must be schooled in the basic duties owed to his family. Derrett's remark here is worth repeating: "After a child reached the age of 5, he began to learn that the society was duty-oriented, not right-oriented . . . no one concerned about his rights; everyone wanted to know his duties and wished to be thought 'worthy to fulfil them.'"[5] So much is contained in Luke's remark that Jesus "went down with [his parents] to Nazareth and was obedient to them" (2:51). This statement shows that Jesus does finally behave in a way that Luke's audience would expect and applaud.

---

4. Burridge, *What Are the Gospels?*, 14–42. In his treatment of "Later Graeco-Roman *bioi*," he identifies the same topics constantly reoccurring (150–72), with a convenient summary on 173–75.

5. Derrett, "An Apt Student's Matriculation," 105.

Encomium and Syncrisis

The practice of syncrisis had been around for many years when Aristotle commented on it, as it was used by contemporary orators. Students of Plutarch's *Lives* are familiar with the genre syncrisis.[6] Moreover, writers of rhetorical handbooks such as Cicero and Quintilian treated it according to the Latin term *comparatio*, that is, as a rhetorical conceptual (thought-) figure.[7] In addition, several studies of ancient rhetoric have exposed modern scholars to this genre,[8] which should make it more familiar to us. There is nothing new or strange here.

In antiquity, as they begin to discuss the genre syncrisis, most responsible authors of rhetorical handbooks begin with a proper definition, for which purpose we have chosen that of the progymnastic author Aphthonius:

> Comparison is a composition made comparative by the process of placing side by side with the subject that which is greater or equal to it. And it is necessary for those making a comparison either to place fine things beside good things or worthless things beside worthless things or small things beside the greater.[9]

The progymnasmata not only contain a clear definition of syncrisis, but provide students with conventional ways for its construction.

Because syncrisis is a favored genre used by Luke, we should give it more attention. Progymnastic authors consider syncrisis as a genre logically distinct from encomium, but in fact, in description of and rules for a syncrisis, these authors instruct students to make a comparison *out of the very topics of an encomium*. For example, at the end of his discourse on encomium, Aphthonius urges a writer to compose a comparison.[10] Moreover, he goes on to say in his specific treatment of the genre syncrisis, that a comparison is a "double encomium": "As a whole, syncrisis is a double

---

6. Lamour, "Making Parallels," but especially the introductory materials on pages 4157–73; Russell, "On Reading Plutarch's *Lives*"; and Stadter, "Plutarch's Comparison of Pericles and Fabius Maximus."

7. Martin, "Progymnastic Topic Lists."

8. Attridge, "The Uses of Antithesis in Hebrews 8–10"; more recently, Neyrey, "Syncrisis and Encomium." On syncrisis in Luke, see O'Fearghail, *Introduction to Luke–Acts*, 33–36.

9. Aphthonius, "The *Preliminary Exercises* of Aphthonius the Sophist," 31R, quoted in Kennedy, trans., *Progymnasmata*.

10. Aphthonius, "The *Preliminary Exercises* of Aphthonius the Sophist," 22R, quoted in Kennedy, trans., *Progymnasmata*.

encomion or <a double> invective or a speech made up of encomion <and invective>."¹¹ Aelius Theon explains this: "Whenever we compare persons we shall first put side by side their good birth and education and excellence of their offspring and the offices they have held and their reputation and the condition of their bodies and other bodily and external good that we mentioned earlier in discussing encomia."¹² Aphthonius put it simply: "You should elaborate comparison with the same headings as encomion."¹³ Therefore, the topics to be compared are not miscellaneous or esoteric, but the common and conventional ones used in encomia and in *bioi*.

Encomium, Syncrisis, and Luke's Ethos of Jesus

Inasmuch as the establishment of an ethos in many cases is achieved by means of progymnastic genres, we will briefly consider what Luke says about the ethos of Jesus by means of the genre syncrisis or comparison. Many have spoken about the extended comparison/contrast between John and Jesus in Luke 1–3, and so this conversation is hardly new.

As well as Luke constructs an ethos for Jesus and himself, he must establish one for John, since John exercises public voice. Only part of that syncrisis appears here as evidence that this progymnastic genre is used in establishing the ethos of Jesus, namely, the comparison of Zechariah and Mary. As significant a figure as John is (origins, role and status), so Jesus is all the more superior. This comparison is necessarily presented there as part of Luke's construction of an ethos for Jesus. But a comparison of Zechariah and Mary would be misleading, since Luke is more interested in their children than in the parents themselves.

---

11. Aphthonius, "The *Preliminary Exercises*," 31R, quoted in Kennedy, trans., *Progymnasmata*.

12. Aelius Theon, "The Exercises of Aelius Theon," 113 quoted in Kennedy, trans., *Progymnasmata*.

13. Aphthonius, "The *Preliminary Exercises*," 31R, quoted in Kennedy, trans. *Progymnasmata*.

Zechariah, Gabriel, and John (1:8–20)	Mary, Gabriel, and Jesus (1:26–39)
When he was serving as priest before God and he was chosen by lot . . . to enter the sanctuary of the Lord and offer incense . . . Then **there appeared to him an angel of the Lord**, standing at the right side of the altar of incense.	In the sixth month **the angel Gabriel was sent by God** to a town in Galilee called Nazareth, to a virgin engaged to a man whose name was Joseph, of the house of David. The virgin's name was Mary. And he came to her and said, "Greetings, favored one! The Lord is with you."
When Zechariah saw him, **he was terrified; and fear overwhelmed him**. But the angel said to him, "**Do not be afraid** . . .	But **she was much perplexed by his words and pondered what sort of greeting this might be**. The angel said to her, "**Do not be afraid** . . .
Your wife Elizabeth will **bear you a son, and you will name him John** . . . **he will be great** in the sight of the Lord."	. . . **you will conceive in your womb and bear a son, and you will name him Jesus. He will be great** . . .
Zechariah said to the angel, "**How will I know that this is so? For I am an old man, and my wife is getting on in years.**" The angel replied, "I am Gabriel . . . and I have been sent to speak to you and to bring you this good news."	Mary said to the angel, "**How can this be, since I am a virgin?**" The angel said to her, 'The Holy Spirit will come upon you, and the power of the Most High will overshadow you; therefore the child to be born will be holy; he will be called Son of God."
But now, **because you did not believe my words**, which will be fulfilled in their time, you will become mute, unable to speak, until the day these things occur."	Then Mary said, **"Here am I, the servant of the Lord; let it be with me according to your word."**

These points of similarity are well-known to scholars, but it is difficult to find any who perceive this as a syncrisis or comparison rather than mere parallels. Moreover, it is equally rare for any to appreciate this syncrisis as one between encomiastic origins, namely, the origins of John and Jesus. But for those familiar with rhetoric, the excellence of the Son who will be named Jesus is clearly superior to the noble character named John. Hardly parallel, they are compared.

But with insight, much more can be said about these data when the John-Jesus comparisons are considered in terms of the common biblical form of a commissioning story. The advantage of reading Luke 1 in this light is that it makes us focus on the central content and therefore the purpose of the comparison, namely, the commissioning of John and Jesus, which are also clearly contrasted.[14] What Luke is comparing and contrasting is the role and status of John with that of Jesus.

The Form of a Commissioning Story: John and Jesus Compared

The following figure contains in the left column the conventional elements of a commissioning form, which occurs with regularity in the Scriptures. The middle column indicates how the commissioning of John in 1:5–25 is structured according the elements of the model, and the right column does the same for the commissioning of Jesus in 1:26–38.

---

14. See Hubbard, *The Matthean Redaction*; and Hubbard, "Commissioning Stories in Luke–Acts"; see also Mullin, "The New Testament Commission Form." Brown (*The Birth of the Messiah*, 629–31) acknowledges the scholarship on the form but prefers to name it "The Annunciation Pattern," which reflects his ambivalence about the use and importance of it. On the one hand, he is considerably focused on the figure of Mary, insisting "that the annunciation of Jesus' birth in Luke . . . [was arguably] a type of commissioning of Mary as the first Christian disciple." But he more wisely says later, "That most of the verses in Luke 1:26–38 concern Jesus (what he will do; who he was) and that the annunciation scene is prefaced to a Gospel about Jesus should make it evident that the primary purpose of this scene is not mariological."

Making a Rhetorical Ethos for Jesus

	Commissioning of John (1:8–22)	Commissioning of Jesus (1:26–38)
Setting	Jerusalem temple, altar of incense	village of Nazareth
Confrontation	Angel appeared . . . he was terrified.	Angel appeared . . . she was much perplexed.
Reassurance	"Do not be afraid"	"Do not be afraid"
Commission	"Your wife will bear you a son, and you will name him John. . . . *he will be great* . . . He must never drink wine or strong drink; even before his birth he will be filled with the Holy Spirit. He will turn the people of Israel to the Lord their God. With the spirit and power of Elijah he will go before him, to turn the hearts of parents to their children, and the disobedient to the wisdom of the righteous, to make ready a people prepared for the Lord."	"You will conceive in your womb and bear a son, and you will name him Jesus. *He will be great* . . . and will be called the Son of the Most High; and the Lord God will give to him the throne of his ancestor David. He will reign over the house of Jacob forever, and of his kingdom there will be no end."
Objection	"How will I know this is so? For I am an old man, and my wife is getting on in years."	"How can this be, since I am a virgin?"
Reassurance	"I am Gabriel. I stand in the presence of God, and I have been sent to speak to you and to bring you this good news."	"The Holy Spirit will come upon you, and the power of the Most High will overshadow you; therefore the child to be born will be holy; he will be called Son of God."
Sign	"When he did come out, he could not speak to them, and they realized that he had seen a vision in the sanctuary."	"Your relative Elizabeth in her old age has also conceived a son; and this is the sixth month for her who was said to be barren."

The advantage of reading these comparative stories according to this familiar biblical form lies in its immediate focus on the rhetorical function of the stories, namely, the commissioning of both John and Jesus. Both figures are ascribed by God's angel with a particular role and status. John will not be a priest, but a prophet in the mold of Elijah; Jesus, however, will be a king, a descendent of David. John's status, of course, is very high because of his role; but the status of Jesus surpasses his because kings are more honorable than prophets (or priests). John's role, moreover, has both a beginning and an ending; when in Luke 3:20 he is finished speaking and acting in the power of Elijah, John exits stage left, except for sending messengers to Jesus (7:18–23). Jesus's role, in contrast, will never end, for "of his kingdom there will be no end" (1:33). And after the theophany in 3:21–22, Jesus begins to act according to this role and status. Knowing the form of a commissioning story, then, allows both author and audience to focus on the key element in each story: the heavenly commissioning of the prophet John and of the king Jesus, and their relative statuses.

This syncrisis, moreover, undoubtedly becomes part of the ethos Luke is constructing for Jesus. The form itself is known, the mode of its presentation is evident, and the rhetorical purpose is clear. Thus, Luke is using one more genre from the progymnasmata, itself conventional and clear, in the construction of the ethos of Jesus.

Summary and Conclusions

Inasmuch as this chapter has argued that Jesus was ascribed an ethos suitable for a person to exercise public voice, we need to assess the extent to which this was done in Luke 1–4 and how successfully. By success we mean that Luke appreciated the need for such an authorization and also knew the appropriate rhetorical ways to achieve it. The endurance and popularity of his Gospel also testifies to his success. What, then, did Luke do?

1. In this chapter we gathered data on the rhetoric Luke employed, on what his audience would have expected from him rhetorically, and on how his audience would have understood his rhetoric. Conventionality exists simultaneously in what techniques a writer uses and in what his audience will understand. Rhetoric could hardly be esoteric if it was crafted to persuade audiences.

2. Luke's rhetorical training began with rhetorical handbooks called progymnasmata. As he progressed in his ability to write prose, he mastered the genres of encomium and syncrisis.

3. Luke used these two genres in service of his major rhetorical task at the beginning of his narrative to establish an ethos for Jesus, so that when Jesus appears as a mature adult in Luke's Gospel, he will have

Making a Rhetorical Ethos for Jesus

authority for public voice. Jesus in Luke 1–2 may only be a babe, infant, and boy, but it is here that the foundations of Jesus's ethos are laid.

4. Luke makes his ethos for Jesus by relentless attention of Jesus's origins, as progymnastic encomia instruct. Luke heralds Jesus' geographical origins (Bethlehem) and generational ones (parents, ancestors, tribe, and genealogy). In this Luke is closely following the description of and instructions on the topic of origins found in the rules for an encomium. Plutarch's connection of generational origins and public voice proves this to be so: "A goodly treasure, then, is honorable birth, and *such a man may speak his mind freely*" (*Mor.* 1, italics added).

5. A proper ethos, moreover, includes other topics from the progymnastic encomium, namely, nurture and training, and comparison with other honorable persons.

6. Luke's literary mechanics for establishing Jesus's ethos lie in his repeated ascription of honor to Jesus, that is, his role and status, which occur because the **Sender-of-Senders** repeatedly sends **messages** by means of authorized **Channels**. All **messages** progressively ascribe to Jesus the highest possible roles and statuses. These communications, then, function to create the ethos of one who will mature and legitimately have public voice.

7. Without recognition of the rhetorical conventions for a proper ethos, it is hard to see how modern readers of Luke would understand what the evangelist is doing in the first four chapters of his narrative. Even if individual pieces are occasionally appreciated, without a sense of the rhetorical whole, the purpose of Luke 1–4 is hard to grasp. Occasional chords in a musical score need a full melody to make sense.

8. There is an evident argument, therefore, that Luke concerns himself with establishing an ethos for Jesus to have public voice, which he does according to ancient conventions—conventions that both Luke and his audience know. Luke, the accomplished rhetorician, knows what is needed, and he establishes the authority of Jesus for public voice according to the rhetorical conventions that he knows and his audience expects.

CHAPTER 7

Luke's Own Ethos

ALL STUDENTS OF LUKE's Gospel have greatly benefitted from the scholarship on the prologue of Luke.[1] In particular, our critical reading of it advances when we consider it in relationship with prologues in ancient literature. Many excellent studies have been conducted on the prologue itself, namely, those of Cadbury,[2] van Unnik,[3] Fitzmyer,[4] Dillon,[5] Du Plessis,[6] and Moessner.[7] Other scholars have endeavored to describe the relationship of the prologue to the rest of Luke's Gospel and even to Acts of the Apostles.[8] The odds do not favor another exegetical investigation, unless different questions are asked about Luke 1:1–4 that might open up new avenues of investigation.

We propose to study the Lukan prologue in the light of classical rhetoric, which in this case consists of the following. First, inasmuch as the prologue begins Luke's narrative, it might be studied in terms of the conventional ways orations and writings traditionally begin (i.e., ethos

---

1. Alexander, "Luke's Preface"; Alexander, *The Preface to Luke's Gospel*; Robbins, "Prefaces in Greco-Roman Biography and Luke–Acts."
2. Cadbury, "Commentary on the Preface of Luke"; and Cadbury, "The Knowledge Claimed in Luke's Preface."
3. Van Unnik, "Once More St. Luke's Prologue."
4. Fitzmyer, *The Gospel according to Luke I–IX*, 290–302.
5. Dillon, "Previewing Luke's Project from His Prologue."
6. Du Plessis, "Once More: The Purpose of Luke's Prologue."
7. Of particular note are the works of Moessner, including "'Eyewitnesses,' 'Informed Contemporaries,' and 'Unknowing Inquirers'"; Moessner, "The Appeal and Power of Poetics"; and Moessner, "The Triadic Synergy of Hellenistic Poetics."
8. Brown, "The Role of the Prologues"; and Schneider, "Zur Bedeutung von καθεξῆς im lukanischen Doppelwerk"; O'Fearghail, *Introduction to Luke–Acts*.

and pathos). Second, it should be examined more carefully according to the traditional criteria for composing a proper ethos (the speaker's knowledge, virtue, and goodwill). Third, as many historians are wont to present themselves in their prologues in comparison with other writers, we should consider how Luke himself conducts a rhetorical syncrisis, that is, a comparison of his labors with those of other writers. And finally, what can study of Luke's rhetorical style tell us about his suitability to write about Jesus?

A Proper Beginning: Ethos and Pathos

As we saw earlier, orations and prose writings must have a proper beginning. This beginning focused on the presentation of the speaker or writer, who was well informed about his topic, who was of virtuous character, and who would tell the truth to his audience, whether pleasant or not. Thus, the speaker's ethos, which is the first order of business in the exordium, must be clear and persuasive. Moreover, while Aristotle indicated that *pooimium/exordium* for each type of rhetoric (forensic, deliberative, epideictic) will vary depending upon the rhetorical situation and the needs of the speaker (*Rhet.* 3.14.1–7), he stated "the forms of exordia ... are derived from the speaker, the hearer, the subject, and the opponent" (*Rhet.* 3.14.7). Concerning the speaker, Aristotle says further, "The object of an appeal to the hearer is to make him well disposed or to arouse his indignation ... As for rendering the hearers tractable, *everything will lead up to it if a person wishes, including the appearance of respectability*, because *respectable* persons command more attention" (*Rhet.* 3.14.7, italics added). So, an exordium focuses on the presentation of the speaker, that is, his ethos. And so, we begin to read Luke's work by examining his own beginning, which in this case is his prologue.

In discussing means of persuasion, Aristotle enumerates three kinds: (1) one depending on the character of the speaker (*ethos*); (2) another which puts the hearer in a certain frame of mind (*pathos*);[9] and (3) yet another based on the speech/writing itself (*logos*) (*Rhet.* 1.2.4). "Character" (*ethos*), Aristotle claims, "is the most effective means of proof" (*Rhet* 1.2.5). And later Aristotle takes ample time to describe "the nature of the characters of men [*ēthē*] according to their emotions [*pathē*], habits, ages, and fortunes" (*Rhet.* 2.9.12). Thus he admits, "all men are willing to listen to

---

9. Several studies of ethos and pathos are worth considering: Gill, "The Ēthos/Pathos Distinction"; and DiCicco, *Paul's Use of Ethos*.

speeches which harmonize with their own character and to speakers who resemble them" (*Rhet.* 2.13.16). Moreover, attention to these three kinds of proofs is generally found at the beginning of a speech (or writing).

The appreciation of these classical proofs allows us to read Luke 1:1–4 in a particular way. First of all, Luke constructs his own ethos, establishing himself as a competent and reliable author. Second, he aims to create in his audience (i.e., Theophilus) the feeling that he is offering him an assured and correct version about which he has thus far received mere instruction. Luke wishes to create the emotion of security that cancels out its opposite. Third, Luke's narrative about Jesus is solidly based on various types of testimony, which is central to a speaker or writer's trustworthiness.

The advantages of reading Luke 1:1–4 in this rhetorical way are manifold. On the one hand, the recognition of the kinds of proof, especially ethos and pathos, is rooted in ancient rhetoric, and so does not depend on a modern idea of how an oration or writing should begin. Moreover, their rhetorical contents are suitably applicable to Luke 1:1–4, with the particular advantage of instructing modern scholars to observe what mode of persuasion Luke is using, which made sense in his time. And reading Luke 1:1–4 in this way urges us to consider the character of Theophilus, what emotions in him Luke seeks to invoke, and the possible reasons for them.

A Proper Ethos

We began discussing a rhetorical ethos in the last chapter, with a focus on how it is traditionally formed. Since *asphaleia* (full truth) is Luke's aim, we focus here on how Luke's presentation of himself, and thus of his work, serves to establish that. Indeed, Luke must present himself to an audience (Theophilus and others) to answer certain immediate questions: Who is speaking or writing? What is he saying? And why? What credentials does he have to warrant anyone paying him attention? We turn again to classical rhetoric to learn how these questions were answered. Construction of an ethos belongs at the beginning of a speech or writing; further, ethos construction happens not only in sequence in the exordium, but also with an ear toward the importance behind the qualities that make up an ethos, because by an ethos a speaker or writer must establish his credentials.[10]

10. Other ancient authors drew from encomiastic topics that spoke to a person's honor and status: "He often makes his client's character appear *trustworthy by referring to the circumstances of his life and his parentage,* and often again by describing his past

Aristotle, who left nothing to chance, described the essential qualities of a proper ethos as an effective means of persuasion. "[T]he speaker should show himself to be possessed of certain qualities and that his hearers should think that he is disposed in a certain way toward them" (*Rhet* 2.1.3). He then enumerates these qualities:

> For the orator to produce conviction three qualities are necessary . . . These qualities are good sense [*phronēsis*], virtue [*aretē*] and goodwill [*eunoia*] . . . These qualities are all that are necessary, so that the speaker who appears to possess all three will necessarily convince his hearers. (*Rhet.* 2.1.6–7)

Therefore, in regard to the ethos of a speaker, we must consider more closely the things that induce belief as the ancient rhetoricians understood them. For example, (1) *phronēsis* means that the speaker *knows what he is talking about*; (2) *aretē* refers to his character and his excellences; and finally, (3) *eunoia* expresses the conviction, not only that he is well-disposed to his hearers, but that he will give them his best advice for their own benefit."

A Well-Informed Author

"Good sense" for Aristotle covered both practical wisdom (*phronēsis*) and philosophy (*sophia*) (*Rhet.* 1.9.27). In his *Rhetorica*, Aristotle has little to say about philosophy/wisdom, and only a bit more about practical wisdom, such as, "Practical wisdom is a virtue of reason, which enables men to come to a wise decision in regard to good and bad things" (*Rhet.* 1.9.13). Other rhetoricians, however, discuss it in ways useful for our task. For example, in *Rhetorica ad Herrenium*, the author defines it in a way worth our attention.

> We shall be using the topics of Wisdom if we compare advantages and disadvantages, counseling the pursuit of the one and the avoidance of the other; if we urge a course in a field in which we have a technical knowledge of the ways and means whereby each detail should be carried out; or if we recommend some policy in a matter whose history we can recall either from direct experience or hearsay—in this instance we can easily persuade our hearers to the course we wish by adducing the precedent. (*Rhet. ad Her.* 3.3.4)

---

actions and purposes" (Diogenes Laertius, *Lysias* 19.3–4, in Hicks, trans., *Lives of Eminent Philosophers*, 1:150; italics added).

By What Authority?

This is confirmed by the remarks of another rhetorician, Menander Rhetor: "Under wisdom, you should praise his legal experience, education, foresight, capacity for clear decisions about present needs . . . critical understanding of orators, ability to judge the whole sense of the subject from the prooemium" (*Treatise* II.415.26—416.4). What constitutes wisdom may be summarized as follows:

1. judgment of what is good or evil, what is desirable and to be chosen or to be avoided, what is advantageous or disadvantageous;
2. practical and expert knowledge of what is useful, even technical knowledge of the ways and means to achieve something;
3. ability to recommend a policy, based on history and experience;
4. memory and experience and acuteness to give good counsel; ability to persuade by adducing precedents.

A Virtuous Author

It is tempting to cite the four canonical virtues as the rhetorical meaning of *aretē*, but that would unfortunately exclude the fundamental understanding of virtue as a form of excellence. But Aristotle offers this definition: "Virtue [*aretē*], it would seem, is a faculty of providing and preserving good things, a faculty *productive* of many and great *benefits*, in fact of all things in all cases" (*Rhet.* 1.3–5, italics added). In a subsequent place, when Aristotle formally discusses virtues, he offers this: "It belongs to wisdom to take counsel, to judge the goods and evils and all things that are desirable and to be avoided, to use all the available goods finely, to behave rightly in society, to observe due occasions, to employ both speech and action with sagacity . . . Memory and experience and acuteness are each of them either a consequence or a concomitant of wisdom; or some of them are as it were subsidiary causes of wisdom, as for instance experience and memory, others as it were parts of it, for example good counsel and acuteness" (*Virtues and Vices* 4.1–2).

To be sure, the components of virtue are "justice, courage, self-control," but *aretē* has to do with *benefitting* others. Frederick W. Danker et al. refine this by defining it as an "uncommon character worthy of praise, excellence of character," which encourages us to consider it as an "exceptional civic virtue."[11] The meaning of *aretē* can also be gleaned from its synonyms:

---

11. BDAG, 130.

> Finally, whatever is true, whatever is honorable, whatever is just, whatever is pure, whatever is pleasing, whatever is commendable, if there is any excellence and if there is anything worthy of praise, think about these things. (Phil 4:8)

The virtue of an author, then, expresses his concern for honor and benevolence.

The Goodwill of the Author

Although we know how a man's virtue may be broadly understood as benevolence, that noble quality became the substance of what Aristotle understood as the goodwill that an orator or speaker must display. Benevolence (*charis*) seems to express goodwill.

> The persons towards whom men feel *benevolent*, and for what reasons, and in what frame of mind, will be clear when we have defined what favor is. Let it be taken to be the feeling in accordance with which one who has it is said *to render a service to one who needs it*, not in return for something nor in the interest of him who renders it, but *in that of the recipient*. And the favor will be great if the recipient is in pressing need, or if the service or the times and circumstances are important or difficult, or if the benefactor is the only one, or the first who has rendered it, or has done so in the highest degree. (*Rhet.* 2.7.1–3, my italics)[12]

In another place, Aristotle spreads out the criteria for a person being labeled noble, which has bearing on our understanding of what is meant by benevolence and goodwill. We have taken the liberty to highlight the beneficial and honorable aspects, which correspond to what is called goodwill in other rhetorical places. In Aristotle, moreover, these aspects of being noble pertain more to the political or social institution rather than that of kinship.

> Things for which the rewards are honor are good [*kala*], especially those that *bring honor* rather than money . . . those things that a man does *not do for his own sake*; things which are absolutely good, which a man has done *for his country*, while *neglecting his own interests*; and things good by nature and that are *not benefits*

---

12. The tags "the *only* one, of the *first* who has done it, or has done so *in the highest degree*" indicate someone or something that is unique. On this, see Neyrey, "'First,' 'Only'"; Neyrey, *An Encomium for Jesus*, 163, 167, 184–86.

> to him, for such things are *done for their own sake* ... and whatever works are done for *the sake of others* (for they have less of the self); and successes gained *for others*, but *not for the self* and for those who have *conferred benefits* (for that is just); and *acts of kindness* (for they are not directed to oneself) ... And those that give *pleasure to others* more than to oneself; thus, the just and justice are honorable. (*Rhet.* 1.9.16–23, my italics)

A person of goodwill will act benevolently and altruistically to another, acting on behalf of another and not for his own benefit.

Luke's Own Proper Ethos

When we apply the three criteria for a proper ethos to Luke's presentation of himself in his prologue, we find considerable correspondence between what is prescribed in rhetoric and Luke's actual account of himself.

Luke's Knowledge

No conversation can begin without careful appreciation of the recent articles of David Moessner on Luke 1:1–4. His research has been exceptionally thorough and cogently argued, a singular contribution to any study of Luke's prologue. In his first article,[13] Moessner focuses on Josephus's understanding of the technical term *parakoloutheō*, an investigation concerned with proper historiography from that time. In the second article, Moessner considers the remarks of Dionysius of Halicarnassus on the rhetorical importance of "arrangement" in an historical composition.[14] These two studies are themselves in conversation with a century of scholarship on Luke's prologue,[15] accepting some things, but correcting others. Moessner's scholarship should be taken as the new benchmark for further commentary on Luke 1:1–4. Inasmuch as readers should consult Moessner's work themselves, we need only use his scholarship to investigate here what Luke knows.

---

13. Moessner, "'Eyewitnesses,' 'Informed Contemporaries,' and 'Unknowing Inquirers.'"

14. Moessner, "The Triadic Synergy of Hellenistic Poetics."

15. The record his Moessner's research may be found in the initial footnote of Moessnser, "'Eyewitnesses,' 'Informed Contemporaries,' and 'Unknowing Inquirers,'" 105.

Luke's Own Ethos

Luke knows that he has predecessors—"many," in fact—whose intent was to write an orderly narrative. "Many"[16] need not mean anything more than "some." From modern scholarship, we think that these authors/sources include Mark, a Sayings Source, and special Lukan materials. Luke at least claims to be familiar or acquainted with "many" of them. He knows, moreover, that these "many" produced a narrative in some sort of order or arrangement (*epexeirēsan anatachasthai diagēsin*). He knows also the content of these previous labors, that is, "the events that have come to fruition among us" (*peri tōn peplērophoremenōn en hēmin pragmatōn*, my trans.). Luke knows their pedigree, that they are "just as from the beginning those who were eyewitnesses and assistants handed on to us" (my trans.). Luke is not saying that he belongs in that primitive group, but only that he knows it was the source and transmission of what he knows. Then he knew that it was his turn to write, because he was so very well and continuously informed. Moessner has convincingly labored to secure for *parakolouthakoti* the meaning of one who has stayed actively informed about both the events and their significance. But, argues Moessner, Luke is *not* doing research into *the past* as though he was ignorant of those matters and needs to *inquire*.

Furthermore, Luke clearly demonstrates that he has a certain level of education needed to compose his prologue. He knows the conventions of historiography[17] and follows them both in terms of what he said (technical terms) and how he says it (an elegant periodic sentence). Although some only note the infrequency of Luke's preface vocabulary in the rest of the New Testament, others inform us that it is unusual only to those unfamiliar with comparable technical terms found in Hellenistic historiography.[18] Entering through this door, we observe that Luke knows of the relative reliability of those who were "eyewitness," "assistants," and "those informed" (my trans.) He knows, moreover, what constitutes reliability according to the canons of

---

16. Bauer, "*POLLOI* Luk 1,1"; Fitzmyer, *The Gospel according to Luke I–IX*, 63–66, 291.

17. In addition to Cadbury, "Commentary on the Preface of Luke," 499–510, see van Unnik, "Once More St. Luke's Prologue." This study consolidates his extensive research in the "Corpus Hellenisticum," from which he provides numerous and persuasive parallels for the controversial terms debated in other commentaries on the prologue. In particular, he points out many technical terms found in ancient histories (i.e. *polloi*, *diēgēsin*, *pragmata*, and *parēkolouthēkoti*), with the result that his readings are closer to ancient rhetoric than those of most other commentators.

18. In addition to Cadbury, "Commentary on the Preface of Luke," one must include the article of van Unnik, "Once More St. Luke's Prologue." His study itself consolidates

Hellenistic historiography.[19] Extrapolating from this examination of Luke's rhetoric and historical skill, we posit for him an education that qualified him for composing prose at this high level of sophistication.

Thus, in answer to what Luke knows, we must include: (1) a constant and accurate following of matters about which he writes; (2) an appropriate knowledge of and appreciation for the works of his predecessors, both oral and written; and (3) a sophisticated knowledge of Hellenistic historiography. His literary abilities go a long way to assuring both his clarity and reliability.[20] And so, he is learned in terms of rhetoric and its ways of persuasion.

Luke's Virtue

One might consider Luke and virtue in two ways, either in terms of the general meaning of *virtue* or according to its components, such as the four canonical virtues. Luke would present himself to Theophilus as broadly virtuous in character by writing for him an orderly account so that he would have confidence and surety, a benevolent act. According to what Luke says in 1:1-4, he seeks only to benefit Theophilus, and apparently seeks nothing in return. Admittedly the prologue is modest in size, but working from what it contains, Luke seeks to benefit another, not himself.

According to the canonical components of *aretē*, we find that Luke alludes to two virtues: (1) courage (labor, endurance, perseverance), and (2) justice (he gives his predecessors their due). We should not expect to find these specific terms used but rather to see their manifestation.[21] Each ca-

---

19. Van Unnik ("Once More St. Luke's Prologue," 13, italics added) offers a persuasive distinction between information had by the author and observations by others who were at the scene, and from reliable sources. He quotes Thucydides:

> As regards the material facts of the war, I have not been content [to rely] on casual informants or my own imagination. Where I have not been an eye-witness myself, I have investigated with the utmost accuracy attainable every detail that I have taken at second hand. (*Hist.* 1.22.2)

This all reflects the proverb found in Herodotus: "The ears are less trustworthy for men than the eyes" (1.8).

20. Moessner, "The Appeal and Power of Poetics."

21. Aristotle instructs: "Use the description instead of the name of a thing ... use metaphors and epithets by way of illustration" (*Rhet.* 3.6.1-3); Menander Rhetor urges: "Do not simply state virtues — e.g., 'He is just' — but treat the topic by considering the opposite: he is not unjust, nor irascible, nor inaccessible, not judging by favoritism, not a taker of bribes" (*Treatise* I.416.5-17, *Menander Rhetor*).

Luke's Own Ethos

nonical virtue, moreover, might be recognized by its own components and synonyms. In regard to courage, Luke presents himself acting diligently, both in his own work and in his report about what others wrote. Although courage is commonly linked with battle and facing death, it also has a more domesticated meaning, as Cicero states:

> Courage is the quality by which one undertakes dangerous tasks and endures hardships. Its parts are confidence, patience, perseverance... Confidence is the quality by which the spirit has placed great trust in itself with a resolute hope of success. Patience, a willing and sustained endurance of difficult and arduous tasks for a noble and useful end. Perseverance, a firm and abiding persistence in a well-considered plan of action. (*Inv.* 2.163)[22]

Luke claims that he labored with care and accuracy (*akribôs*); he made careful investigations to assure that his writing was carefully done, a mark of endurance. Although Luke does not say so, his labor and perseverance were not easily achieved, nor quickly—marks of patience and endurance.

Justice, likewise, means more than retribution or reward. The following comment by a rhetorician close in time to Cicero spreads out for us a broad understanding of justice.

> We will be using the topics of justice if we show that it is proper to repay the well-deserving with gratitude... if we urge that faith ought zealously to be kept; if we say that the laws and customs of the state ought especially to be preserved; if we contend that alliances and friendships should scrupulously be honored; if we make it clear that the duty imposed by nature toward parents, gods, and fatherland must be religiously observed. (*Rhet. ad Her.* 3.3.4)

This definition urges us to note the respect Luke has for the "many" and for the eyewitnesses and ministers whose contribution he notes. He gives them their just due. A full rendering of this must wait until we consider Luke 1:1–4 as a syncrisis or comparison, but Luke does give them proper respect for what they achieved. Not harsh criticism, for he acknowledges them as worthy of comparison. His labors to do proper research sound very similar

---

22. Aristotle, too, appreciated that courage was not restricted to facing battle and death: "It also belongs to courage to labor and endure and play a manly part. Courage is accompanied by confidence and bravery and daring, and also by perseverance and endurance" (*On Virtues and Vices* 4.4). The same appears in *Rhet. ad Her.*: "When we invoke as a motive for a course of action steadfastness in courage, we shall make it clear that men out to follow and strive after noble and lofty actions" (3.3.5).

to "faith ought zealously to be kept . . . laws and customs ought especially to be preserved."

Luke's Goodwill

Although all agree that Luke's purpose in writing is expressed in 1:4, few agree as to what that purpose was. Schuyler Brown's article on the purpose of Luke's prologue lists five different reasons why Luke wrote.[23] But according to the criteria for a proper ethos, at a minimum Luke's fundamental goodwill should be considered. Minimally, Luke is doing something that benefits another rather than himself; he is doing an act of kindness to others, and is conferring a benefit to them. Without doubt Luke displays considerable goodwill to Theophilus (and others) by his labors, offering his account to them without expecting any return.

Syncrisis

But one avenue of research seems not to have attracted much attention, namely, the consideration of Luke 1:1–4 in terms of the progymnastic genre syncrisis or comparison.[24] That is, Luke's preface apparently compares and contrasts what he is writing with the products of previous authors. Luke must, after all, argue why Theophilus or anyone else would want to hear what Luke is saying. What advantage does his work have over the others? We introduced previously the progymnastic topic syncrisis, to which readers might want to return.

The practice of syncrisis had been already current for many years when Aristotle commented on it.[25] And it continued through time, until

---

23. Brown, "The Role of the Prologues," 100, lists (1) the rehabiltation of Paul, (2) an apology directed to the Roman state, (3) the evangelization of the non-Christian world, (4) the solution to a theological problem, and (5) a defense against heresy.

24. Joseph A. Fitzmyer's commentary on the preface/prologue of Luke began to do this. Scholarship at his time was not well acquainted with rhetoric, much less with the progymnastic genre of *syncrisis*, but this acute scholar constantly observed contrasts between what "the many" had written and Luke's "accurate account." His reading of Luke 1:1–4 stands out because of his cross-referencing to instances of the same vocabulary in both Luke and Acts, which gives his interpretation considerable support. His is the seed which became this current study.

25. "If he does not furnish you with enough in himself, you must compare him with others, as Isocrates used to do . . . And you must compare him with illustrious personages,

rhetorical writers such as Cicero and Quintilian treated it according to the Latin term *comparatio*, that is, as a rhetorical conceptual (thought-) figure.[26] But we find the clearest definition of *syncrisis* and the rule for its construction in the rhetorical handbooks called the progymnasmata. Aphthonius provides the leanest of definitions:

> Comparison is a composition made comparative by the process of placing side by side with the subject that which is greater or equal to it. And it is necessary for those making a comparison either to place fine things beside good things or worthless things beside worthless things or small things beside the greater."[27]

These remarks suffice, since most progymnastic authors repeat the same definition and rules for composing a syncrisis. Since we endeavor to read Luke 1:1–4 correctly as a typical example of one, we must be clear on who might be compared with whom and of what the comparison might consist.

1. *Good and better.* Comparisons compare *good with better,* hence that to which something is compared should not be attacked or discredited. It is banal to compare good with evil, base with noble. As Aphthonius said: "Comparison is made comparative by placing side by side with the subject that which is greater or equal to it . . . fine things beside good things."

2. *Criteria of worth.* Items in a comparison are by no means arbitrary, as the following materials indicate. According to the classical canons for what is noble and honorable, we note Aelius Theon's ten points of comparison.[28] For convenience's sake, they may be resumed as follows: actions judged better are those

---

for it affords ground for amplification, and is noble, if he can be proved better than men of worth" (*Rhet.* 1.9.38–39).

26. Lausburg, *Handbook of Literary Rhetoric*, 755–910; Cicero, *De Orat.* 3.200–203; Quintilian, *Inst. Orat.* 1.8.16; 9.4.117

27. Aphthonius, "Preliminary Exercises of Aphthonius the Sophist," 31R.

28. The full text reads as follows: "After this we shall compare their actions, giving preference to those that are more beautiful [noble] and giving reasons why the good qualities (of one) are more numerous and greater (than those of the other) and more steadfast and more lasting, and preferring things that were done at a more crucial time (and brought great benefit from the doing) and if they had not been done there would have been great harm, and giving preference to things done by choice than by necessity or by chance, and things which few did more than what many did—for common and ordinary things are not very praiseworthy. (Actions are better) which we do with toil rather than easily and which we accomplish beyond (expectations of) our age and

(1) which are more *noble* and have *reasons* for their good qualities,

(2) which are more *numerous* and *greater*,

(3) which are more *steadfast*,

(4) which are more *lasting*,

(5) which were done at a more *crucial time*, and brought *great benefit*,

(6) from which *great harm results* when they have not been done,

(7) which were done *by choice* rather than by necessity or by chance,

(8) which *few* people did more than many, for common and ordinary things are not very praiseworthy,

(9) which were done *with toil*, rather than easily,

(10) which we accomplish *beyond* (expectations of) our *age and ability*.[29]

3. *Actions, unique.* Persons and their actions were typically evaluated in terms of their uniqueness. Uniqueness as a hallmark of honor is found in Aristotle: "[In epideictic] one should also use many kinds of amplification, for example if the subject [of praise] is the *only* one or the *first* or *one of a few* or the one who *most* has done something; for all these things are honorable" (*Rhet.* 1.9.38; see also *Rhet.* 2.7.2; see also Cicero *De Orat.* 2.85.347; and Quintilian *Inst. Orat.* 3.7.16). Aelius Theon stated: "Actions are praised on the basis of the occasion and whether someone did them alone or was the first or when no one else acted, or did more than others or with few helpers or beyond what was characteristic of his age or contrary to expectation or with toils or because they were done very easily or quickly."[30]

Luke and "the Many": Syncrisis in Luke 1:1–4

Luke's rhetorical skill extends beyond the knowledge of how to structure his writing with an exordium and prologue, as well as the other rhetorical

---

(apparent) ability more than when (such actions are ordinarily possible)" (Aelius Theon, "The *Exercises* of Aelius Theon," #113).

29. The list, of course, repeats Aristotle's criteria for what is "noble," mentioned above. It provides one more instance of the existence of classical rhetoric in the time of Luke and other New Testament writers.

30. Aelius Theon, "The *Exercises* of Aelius Theon," #110.

conventions we have noted. He constructs the bulk of his argument in 1:1–4 according to the progymnastic genre known as syncrisis (or comparison). Many have noted that some sort of comparison occurs in Luke 1:1–4, although no one has considered it according to the rhetorical genre syncrisis, especially as this is presented in the progymnasmata. Moreover, judgments on the severity of Luke's comparisons differ, as noted by W. C. Van Unnik.[31] But the degree of difference between critical[32] and moderate judgments will be clarified when one considers the comparisons according to the formal instructions in the genre syncrisis. Previous scholars were simply unfamiliar with certain genres of rhetoric, which absence effects how they read Luke 1:1–4. And so, it seems good to us to give some information on the genre syncrisis.

Although it would be tempting to look for exact comparisons between Luke and his predecessors, it seems better to follow the progymnastic rules for an encomium and set side by side persons, works, and topics, one of which should be the contrast in time.

The **time** factor in the prologue seems to compare two time elements. Despite the temptation to construct a timeline between "eyewitnesses," "many" (writers), and Luke ("and me also"), most exegetes perceive only two, namely, the past and the present. The initial word of the prologue (*epeidēper*) refers to a fact already known (i.e., past events still known). The "many" (*polloi*), who are Luke's predecessors, belong also to the past. These "many" have "collected facts" (*epexeirēsan*) about "events" from the past *(peri tōn peprērophorēmentōn en hēmin pragmatōn)*. Balancing what has already been done is Luke's declaration that it is now his turn, in the present, to research and write.

The **work** of Luke's predecessors may be compared with his own. The "many" have already gathered and collected facts, which they arranged into a "well-ordered, polished work" (*diēgēsin*). W. C. van Unnik cites many parallels from ancient writers that "describe two essential phases in the work of an historian according to Greek theory and practice: first a collection of

---

31. Van Unnik ("Once More St. Luke's Prologue," 15) reported: "According to Klein and Schulz Luke is very critical and wanted to supersede his predecessors; according to others like Haenchen, Delling and von Campenhausen his is more moderate, though they find that a note of dissatisfaction is unmistakable."

32. For a very contemporary assessment of Luke's prologue as critical of its predecessors, see Parsons, *Luke*, 26–31. Parsons, who is well informed about syncrisis, never seems to have considered how Luke may be conducting a comparison with others, not at all denigrating them; see the treatment of syncrisis later in this chapter.

facts, which is followed by a text which puts the collected material into an orderly work."[33] The *diēgēsis*, then, is the final product.

Luke also writes about them, which some have interpreted as criticism of previous works.[34] He is writing a narrative (*diēgēsis*), and he explains his working method. He has done his research, because he has "gotten acquainted" (*parēkolouthēkoti*) with all available information with care and accuracy (*akribōs*) about the known tradition (*pasin*). But what Luke writes is qualified by the adverb *kathechēsē*, which some take to mean "a proper sequence," as the word is used in Acts 11:4, not in a chronological sense but in terms of an idea sequence.

In the rules for making a syncrisis, the rhetorical authors were emphatic that a comparison should be made between something good and something better. It would seem that Luke holds a favorable assessment of what the "many" have previously composed. His writing, however, is better; but in what way? He knows what others have written, and he has gotten acquainted with what has been "preserved" (*paredosan*), namely, what eyewitness saw and communicated and what subsequent preachers (*hypēretai*) preached. This solidifies the contents of the works of "many," inasmuch as it satisfies what ancient historians considered the correct sources for writing history.[35] Luke does not claim to know more facts than others, but to have written an orderly account.[36] Moreover, this newer account will serve a purpose not stated in what the "many" wrote: because of this work, Theophilus may know the "certainty" (*asphaleia*), which stands behind what he has written.

The **purpose** for the writing of the accounts by the "many" and by Luke differ, but not in a derogatory way. The end product of the eyewitness

---

33. Van Unnik ("Once More St. Luke's Prologue," 12–13) cites many classical texts, which include eyewitness of an event, the reports of impartial informants, and finally a polished work. He emphasizes throughout his article the distinction made repeatedly by ancient writers that the eye is superior to the ear.

34. Du Plessis ("Once More: The Purpose of Luke's Prologue," 261–62) argues well about interpreting *diēgēsis* in 1:1. "The fact that Luke also wrote does not suggest criticism on his predecessors or that he disagrees with their labors. This can also be seen in the fact that he compares (*kathôs* i 2) their work with the tradition that he himself had received. It is especially clear from the *ka'moi* (i 3) that Luke does not think in terms of reproach or something similar."

35. Van Unnik, "Once More St. Luke's Prologue," 12–13.

36. In a recent monograph, I have argued that Luke is using the template of an encomium to collect and order his findings according to the conventional topics of an encomium (Neyrey, *An Encomium for Jesus*).

testimony, the preaching of it, the gathering of facts, and the final form of it is surely honorable in many ways. So honorable that Luke himself has consulted them. The previous *diēgēsis* served the purpose of spreading the gospel about Jesus. Luke accepts this but adds another purpose for which he writes. He clearly intends to give security or confidence (*asphaleia*) to what Theophilus already knows in an incomplete manner. Hence Luke claims his writing to be better than what Theophilus was previously taught, because it is more complete or more orderly. Moreover, Luke claims to be presenting his *diēgēsis* with something better than that provided by the "many." Luke presents his material according to a specific "modality," that is, *kathechēs*, an order that is better than previous accounts, because it will present Jesus according to encomiastic topics.³⁷

Luke's **purpose**, moreover, is itself eminently honorable and noble. We noted above Aelius Theon's criterion for labeling someone's behavior as praiseworthy, which criterion makes it superior to that of the person to whom he is compared. He is more noble or honorable when his actions are (a) more noble, (b) more numerous, (c) greater, (d) more steadfast, (e) lasting, (f) done at a more crucial time, (f) the cause of great benefit, and (g) done more by choice than by necessity. Actions are noble that few other people have done, that are done with toil, and that are accomplished beyond expectations of age and ability. Luke's actions qualify as noble, because he produces something better than his predecessors, which is reliable and lasting, which appears opportunely, which is of great benefit (to Theophilus, at least), which Luke chooses to do and with considerable labor and toil, and which few others have done, certainly not as well as he has done. We can claim this noble purpose for Luke according to the conventional criteria for noble and honorable behavior cited by a progymnastic author almost contemporary with Luke. Yet this catalogue of noble actions is itself ancient, articulated earlier by Aristotle, who argues for a conventional understanding of who is honorable and noble.

Evaluating Luke's prologue in terms of the rhetorical genre syncrisis serves several purposes. First, it attests to Luke's literary skill, for he knows this rhetorical genre and follows carefully the rules for making one. Second, he favorably acknowledges his sources, as well as the labor with which he does his task. He is, indeed, knowledgeable about what he writes. His syncrisis with his predecessors serves to establish his credentials for the correctness and accuracy (*asphaleia*) of his writing. And in his syncrisis, he

---

37. Schneider, "Zur Bedeutung von καθεξῆς im lukanischen Doppelwerk," 129–31.

claims to be a noble and honorable author, not that his predecessors were not; but his task and his motives for writing are explicit and honorable.

Luke's Rhetorical Style

One final question might be asked of Luke in regard to his ethos, which establishes him as a competent author. It presumes our recognition of the rhetorical genres and topics we have observed in this book. What is the literary level of Luke's style? Even to ask the question requires us to know something about ancient discussions of style, for which purpose we turn to Cicero *De Oratore*, book 3. Apparently speaking for Cicero, the narrative character Crassus identifies four aspects of style: it must be "correct, lucid, ornate and suitably appropriate" (3.10.37). He then treats each, but not in a clear-cut manner. By "correct" he means the correct use of vocabulary and grammar; "lucid" means that the orator (or writer) is "employing words in customary use that indicate literally the meaning we desire to be conveyed...without ambiguity of language or style" (*De Oratore* 3.10.38–39). "Ornate" means that the communication is embellished in terms of its sentence structure (periodic sentences), and may employ comparison and contrast (syncrisis), and display elegance and appropriateness. "Suitably appropriate" style concerns itself with beginnings and endings and is properly concerned with vocabulary.

The present consideration of Luke's style depends heavily upon the scholarship of two authors, Henry Cadbury and W. C. van Unnik. Cadbury and van Unnik are completely at home in the literary world of antiquity and cite numerous parallels with Luke from ancient literature, which go a long way to clarifying the character of Luke's vocabulary.

As Cadbury and van Unnik indicate, Luke writes correct Greek.[38] Many, however, have found Luke less than lucid in his choice of words.[39] It has been pointed out, however, that many of these critics might themselves be faulted for trying to translate Luke into our own language because they are simply ignorant of the historical and cultural ambiance of Luke's

---

38. Praise from W. C. van Unnik is praise indeed: "He prefaced his gospel with a prologue in good Greek style. But with a special stamp that suited the occasion... Such a prooemium was not indispensable in an historical work... but if it was composed it should ensure the reader's attention by making it clear that the work is important ("Once More St. Luke's Prologue," 18–19).

39. Minear, "Dear Theo," 133.

language.[40] We will return to the matter of Luke's clarity when we consider what was expected of word choice in regard to style. Reading *De Oratore* in terms of correct and lucid style, Cicero's narrative character Crassus never stops demanding that an orator (or writer) "must have read and discussed and handled and debated the whole of the contents of the life of mankind" (3.14.54), in particular "knowledge of facts" (3.14.55) . . . "the fullest possible supply of facts" (3.21.91). Such a competent person will have learned correctness and lucidity in his investigations. Luke claims to have done hard study of all available materials (1:3); and inasmuch as Luke uses language conventional in the writing of history, he should be given credit for learning the professional language appropriate to his writing task.

Consideration of proper ornamentation for a style befitting historical writing proves difficult, as it did even for the ancients. But Crassus attempts an answer: "Well, then, the most ornate speeches are those which take the widest range and which turn aside from the particular matter in dispute to engage in an explanation of the meaning of the general issue, so as to enable the audience to base their verdict . . . on a knowledge of the character of the matter as a whole" (*De Orat.* 3.30.120). Luke has claimed to do just this, when he continued to be acquainted with everything (1:3) so as to provide the best assurance (*asphaleia*) for Theophilus's judgment. If this is a mark of good style, then Luke seems to have intended it and achieved it.

Another aspect of proper ornamentation entails the effort to make a speech convincing, which the narrative character Antonius urged by "explaining something or winning sympathy or arousing emotion" (*De Oratore* 3.27.104–105). This means making a proper *pathos* in the audience or reader, which Luke appears to have attempted by offering Theophilus assurance for what he knows only in part.

We are told, however, that it is even more important to make a comparison, by means of "praise and blame" (laudandi et vituperandi" (*De Oratore* 3.27.105–7). "For," Crassus says, "nothing is more effective for the development and amplification of a speech than to be able to use both of these in the fullest abundance" (*De Oratore* 3.27.105). Previously, when we considered Luke's extensive comparison between himself and his "many" predecessors, we observed that his syncrisis, however, was not denigrating

---

40. Van Unnik remarked, "Not that Luke failed in expressing himself, for one word was not enough for the wise contemporary Theophilus, but we fail to understand him, because his presuppositions are not ours" ("Once More St. Luke's Prologue," 10). His scholarly remedy is to read Luke in the light of his own study of the "Corpus Hellenisticum."

of his predecessors. Nevertheless, syncrisis was part of an elegant and effective style.

Another aspect of style considers the length and complexity of a sentence, which is often called a "periodic sentence."[41] Commentators often recognize Luke's opening remarks as an elegant periodic sentence.[42]

Finally, we return to Luke's choice of words, his diction, or his vocabulary. Ornate style, we are told, should "avoid what is commonplace and hackneyed and employ select and distinguished terms that seem to have some fullness and sonority in them" (*De Oratore* 3.37.150); how beneficial it is to "employ a good and copious vocabulary" (*De Oratore* 3.37.151). As van Unnik warned, modern readers without a fulsome reading of ancient literature, especially history, will inevitably fail to appreciate Luke' highly educated choice of words. Cadbury and van Unnik, in particular, rightly point out how conventional was Luke's choice of words, which are found regularly in ancient historians. Not common, but appropriate. What seems difficult for modern readers to understand was not so for Luke's peers. For example, a simple word like "many" (*polloi*) is a regular rhetorical term in antiquity, a topos.[43] Other words commonly found in ancient historical writings prove to be unique to Luke in the New Testament. Conventions common to classical literature appear only in Luke, such as dedicating a work to someone or employing a formal address of an official. Luke's use of conventional vocabulary and even of technical terms argues that his diction is suitably appropriate to his task; that is, to compose a formal prologue that might stand alongside those in other historical works without embarrassment.

Excursus: Communication Clarification of the Prologue

Who says **what** to **whom**, and **why**?[44] We can only surmise that Luke was of a sufficient status to be well educated in ways suited for public oratory and

---

41. The discussion of a periodic sentence is scattered in Cicero's work: 3.25.96–97; 3.26.103–104; 3.43.171; 3.47.182; 3.49.190.

42. Van Unnik, once more: "He [Luke] did his best, wrote an excellent sentence; he complied with the literary conventions of his time . . . he [did not] spare himself the trouble of writing a master-sentence" ("Once More St. Luke's Prologue," 9).

43. See Bauer, "*POLLOI* Luk.I,1."

44. Alexander, "Luke's Preface in the Context of Greek Preface-Writing" effectively

prose writing. Because we have accurate knowledge about the kind of rhetorical prose that Luke could write,[45] we can conclude that Luke confidently presents himself as a rhetorically educated person of sufficient training, who should speak while others listen. **What** Luke writes is an encomiastic biography for Jesus, which, as he says, is well informed by reliable sources and which he crafts into a better version of what he studied.[46] **To whom?** It is well argued that "excellent Theophilus" is likely a patron, a person of rank and status, a believer, who is worthy of Luke's respectful dedication. **Why** does Luke write? He wants to give Theophilus both accurate and reliable knowledge, a virtuous act on his part, which also serves to honor Jesus, the Christ.

Summary and Conclusions

Luke writes a prologue to his work (1:1–4) for reasons commensurate with the functions of similar ancient prologues. But in doing so, Luke also reflects the rhetorical imperative that an orator or writer present himself as a person who himself deserves to be heard when he communicates. This chapter recognizes that rhetorical purpose and has tried to demonstrate the logical necessity for such in assessing the qualities for an orator or writer to display. These considerations take us well beyond the conventions of writing history and prefaces, and into the realm of rhetoric where specific items are required for trustworthy communication. By taking into account first-century rhetorical conventions that Luke learned as part of his education, the critical analysis of Luke 1:1–4 has been greatly advanced. Rhetorical conventions, moreover, are not mere novelties, but are the essential means

---

asked the same questions, but without reference to communication theory. Her impressive study, however, is incomplete in several ways. First, she focuses exclusively on Luke 1:1–4; second, she seems to disparage handbook rhetoric as well as ancient rhetorical writers (Alexander, Herrenius, Cicero, and Quintilian) as impossible or unsatisfactory education for Luke. What should be added to her scholarship are studies such as Martin, "Progymnastic Topic Lists"; and Neyrey, *An Encomium for Jesus*, chs 1–2, and especially "The Appendix of Rhetorical Studies of Luke–Acts."

45. For a catalogue of what rhetoric Luke knows, as discussed by modern scholars, see Neyrey, *An Encomium for Jesus*, 194–96.

46. Fitzmyer, *Luke I–IX*, 298–99.

for Luke to express himself as an educated person and so that his audience to can hear and appreciate how reliably he writes.

With his own ethos secure, Luke can validly expect his audience to consider him trustworthy in his primary task, that is, writing a narrative about Jesus. His concern to establish an ethos for Jesus in great measure depends on his own trustworthiness, which he must establish immediately in his writing. Whatever constitutes a noble ethos for Jesus depends on Luke's own ethos as an informed, noble, and benevolent author. Therefore, it is hardly optional for Luke to begin his work with the establishment of his own ethos, nor may considerate readers deem a close rhetorical examination of Luke's ethos optional.

1. Inasmuch as Luke knows that he must establish an ethos for Jesus to be accorded public voice, and for John to be accepted as a prophet, Luke also knows that he must establish for himself as author his own ethos. And he knows the conventional ways this is done.

2. Although it may seem obvious to us that an author constructs his ethos at the beginning of his communication, what is obvious is also this convention in classical rhetoric. It is in the exordium, in the initial part of a speech or a piece of prose, that this must be done.

3. Luke seems quite aware of the three qualities for a satisfactory ethos of a communicator: knowledge of the subject, virtuous benevolence to his audience, and goodwill to act on their behalf and not for his own benefit. Luke does not express himself using the technical terms as are found in rhetorical handbooks, but the contents of them are clearly on display.

4. In ancient rhetorical handbooks we find the use of specific and technical terms. In Luke, however, we do not find these terms. But the ancient rhetoricians did not want orators and writers to be so crass in their compositions as to use these terms explicitly. It was expected that authors, orators, and audiences would be sufficiently aware of matters rhetorical that the presence of rhetorical techniques would be evident from their employment.

5. One important element of establishing a rhetorical ethos is comparison of the author's work with those of others. And as we saw, a respectable syncrisis compares what is good with what is better. In

his comparison with "the many," Luke pays respect to them by acknowledging them and consulting them. But he claims that his work is better.

6. Consideration of Luke's style should be based on how it was described in classical rhetoric. Luke acquitted himself well by demonstrating what was expected of an educated author. While assessment of style among modern scholars lends itself to subjectivity, ancient rhetorical authors at least provided some canons that they considered hallmarks of proper style. Recovery of these, while important in themselves, gives us means to evaluate Luke in terms of the rhetoric of his own times.

7. A proper conclusion from this last chapter would be that Luke was educated at a high level in traditional rhetoric, and that he was comparably literate in the secular literature appropriate to his status. And so, after constructing a proper ethos for himself, he may with assurance compose a literary work of sophistication to give comparable assurance to Theophilus.

Bibliography

Alexander, Loveday. "Luke's Preface in the Context of Greek Preface-Writing." *NovT* 28 (1986) 48–74.
———. *The Preface to Luke's Gospel. Literary Convention and Social Context.* SNTSMS 78. Cambridge: Cambridge University Press, 1993.
Anderson, H. "Broadening Horizons. The Rejection at Nazareth Pericope of Luke 4:16–30 in Light of Recent Critical Trends." *Int* 18 (1964) 259–75.
Aphthonius. "The Preliminary Exercises of Aphthonius the Sophist." In *Progymnasmata: Greek Textbooks of Prose Composition and Rhetoric*, translated by George A. Kennedy, 89–127. WGRW 10. Atlanta: SBL, 2003.
Aristotle. *Virtues and Vices.* In *The Athenian Constitution; The Eudemian Ethics; Virtues and Vices*, 488–503. Translated by H. Rackham. LCL 285. Cambridge: Harvard University Press, 1967.
———. *The Art of Rhetoric.* Translated by John Henry Freese. Aristotle in 23 vols., 22. LCL. Cambridge: Harvard University Press, 1975.
Arnold, G. "Eröffnungswendungen in griechischen und lateinischen Schriften." *ZNW* 68 (1977) 123–27.
Attridge, Harold W. "The Uses of Antithesis in Hebrews 8–10." *HTR* 79 (1986) 1–9.
Audet, J.-P. "Autour de la Théologie de Luc I-II." *Sciences Ecclésiastiques* 11 (1959) 409–18.
Barton, Stephen C. *Discipleship and Family Ties in Mark and Matthew.* SNTSMS 80. Cambridge: Cambridge University Press, 1994.
Bassler, Jouette. "Luke and Paul on Impartiality." *Bib* 66 (1986) 546–52.
Bauer, J. "*POLLOI* Luk.I,1." *NovT* 4 (1960) 263–66.
Berlo, David K. *The Process of Communication.* New York: Holt, Rinehart & Winston, 1960.
Black, C. Clifton. "The Rhetorical Form of the Hellenistic Jewish and Early Jewish Sermon: A Response to Lawrence Wills." *HTR* 81 (1988) 1–18.
Bock, Darrell L. *Luke.* Vol. 1, *1—9:50.* 2 vols. Baker Exegetical Commentary on the New Testament 3. Grand Rapids: Baker, 1994.
Boismard, M. E. *St. John's Prologue.* Westminster, MD: Newman, 1957.
Bordieu, Pierre. "The Sentiment of Honour in Kabyle Society." In *Honour and Shame: The Values of Mediterranean Society*, edited by J. G. Peristiany, 191–241. Chicago: University of Chicago Press, 1966.

BIBLIOGRAPHY

Borgen, Peder. "The Son of Man Saying in John 3:13–14." In *Philo, John and Paul: New Perspectives on Judaism and Early Christianity*, 103–20. BJS 131. Atlanta: Scholars, 1987.

Boring, M. Eugene. "Mark 1:1–15 and the Beginning of the Gospel." *Semeia* 52 (1990) 43–81.

Bovon, François. "Le Dieu du Luc." *RSR* 69 (1981) 279–300.

Brown, Raymond E. *The Birth of the Messiah: A Commentary on the Infancy Narratives in Matthew and Luke*. New York: Doubleday, 1993.

———. "Luke's Method in the Annunciation Narrative of Chapter One." In *No Famine in the Land: Studies in Honor of John L. McKenzie*, edited by James W. Flanagan and Anita Weisbrod Robinson, 179–94. Missoula, MT: Scholars, 1975.

Brown, Schuyler. "The Role of the Prologues in Determining the Purpose of Luke–Acts." In *Perspectives on Luke–Acts*, edited by Charles H. Talbert, 99–111. Danville, VA: Association of Baptist Professors of Religion, 1978.

Buchanan, George W. "Apostolic Christology." In *SBLSP 1986*, 172–82.

Bühler, Karl. *Sprachtheorie: Die Darstellungsfunktion der Sprache*. Jena: Fischer, 1934.

Bultmann, Rudolf. "*gignōskō*." In *TDNT* 1 (1964) 704–5.

Burnett, Fred W. "The Undecidability of the Proper Name 'Jesus' in Matthew." *Semeia* 54 (1991) 123–44.

Burridge, Richard A. *What Are the Gospels? A Comparison with Graeco-Roman Biography*. Waco: Baylor University Press, 2018.

Cadbury, Henry J. "Commentary on the Preface of Luke." In *The Beginnings of Christianity*, edited by F. J. Foakes Jackson and Kirsopp Lake, 2:499–510. 5 vols. London: Macmillan, 1920–1933.

———. "The Knowledge Claimed in Luke's Preface." *Expositor* 8 (1922) 401–20.

———. *The Making of Luke–Acts*. Rev. ed. London: SPCK, 1958.

Cicero, Marcus Tullius. *De inventione, De optimo genere oratorum, Topica*. Translated by H. M. Hubble. LCL. Cambridge: Harvard University Press, 1960.

———. *De Oratore*. Edited and translated by E. W. Sutton and H. Rackham. LCL. Cambridge: Harvard University Press, 1942.

———. *Rhetorica ad Herennium*. Translated by Harry Caplan. LCL. Cambridge: Harvard University Press, 1954.

Combrink, H. J. B. "The Structure and Significance of Luke 4:16–30." *Neotestamentica* 7 (1973) 24–48.

Cosgrove, Charles H. "The Divine DEI in Luke–Acts: Investigations into the Lukan Understanding of God's Providence." *NovT* 26 (1984) 168–90.

Dahl, Nils Alstrup. *Jesus in the Memory of the Early Church*. Minneapolis: Augsburg, 1976.

———. "The Neglected Factor in New Testament Theology." *Reflections* 73 (1975) 5–8.

Danker, Frederick W. "The Endangered Benefactor in Luke–Acts." In *SBLSP 1981*, 39–48.

DeMaris, Richard E. "The Baptism of Jesus: A Ritual-Critical Approach." In *The Social Setting of Jesus and the Gospels*, edited by Wolfgang Stegemann et al., 137–57. Minneapolis: Fortress, 2002.

———. *The New Testament in Its Ritual World*. London: Routledge, 2008.

———. "Ritual Studies in the New Testament." In *The New Testament in Its Ritual World*, 1–13. London: Routledge, 2008.

Derrett, J. Duncan M. "An Apt Student's Matriculation (Lk 2,39–52)." *Estudios Biblicos* 58 (2000) 201–22.

Bibliography

———. *Jesus' Audience: The Social and Psychological Environment in Which He Worked.* New York: Seabury, 1974.
DiCicco, Mario M. *Paul's Use of Ethos, Pathos, and Logos in 2 Corinthians 10–13.* Mellen Biblical Press Series 31. Lewiston, NY: Mellen, 1995.
Dillon, Richard J. "Previewing Luke's Project from His Prologue (Luke 1:1–4)." *CBQ* 43 (1981) 205–27.
Dobson, Derek S. *Reading Dreams: An Audience-Critical Approach to the Dreams in the Gospel of Matthew.* LNTS 397. London: T. & T. Clark, 2009.
Dodd, C. H. *The Interpretation of the Fourth Gospel.* Cambridge: Cambridge University Press, 1970.
Dolan, Walter. "Reciprocities in Homer." *CW* 72 (1981) 137–75.
———. "The Unequal Exchange between Glaucus and Diomedes in Light of the Homeric Gift-Economy." *Phoenix* 43 (1989) 1–15.
Dungan, David L., and David L. Cartlidge. *Sourcebook of Texts for the Comparative Study of the Gospels.* Sources for Biblical Study 1. Missoula, MT: Scholars, 1974.
Du Plessis, I. I. "Once More: The Purpose of Luke's Prologue (Lk I 1–4)." *NovT* 16 (1974) 259–71.
Eickelman, Dale F. *The Middle East: An Anthropological Approach.* 2nd ed. Englewood Cliffs, NJ: Prentice Hall, 1989.
Esler, Philip F. *Community and Gospel in Luke–Acts: The Social and Political Motivations of Lucan Theology.* SNTSMS 57. Cambridge: Cambridge University Press, 1987.
Ferneberg, Wolfgang. *Der Markusprolog: Studien zur Formbestimmung des Evangeliums.* SANT 36. Munich: Kösel, 1974.
Fisk, Bruce N. "Synagogue Influence on Paul's Roman Readers." https://www.westmont.edu/~fisk/paulandscripture/FiskSynagogueInfluenceonPaulsRomanReaders.pdf/.
Fitzmyer, Joseph A. *The Gospel according to Luke I–IX.* Anchor Bible 28. Garden City, NY: Doubleday, 1981.
Forbes, Christopher. "Comparison, Self-Praise and Irony: Paul's Boasting and the Conventions of Hellenistic Rhetoric." *NTS* 32 (1986) 1–30.
Freese, John Henry, trans. *The Art of Rhetoric*, by Aristotle. LCL. Cambridge: Harvard University Press, 1975.
Gärtner, Bertil E. "The Pauline and Johannine Idea of 'To Know God' against Hellenistic Background." *NTS* 14 (1968) 209–31.
Gibbs, J. M. "Mark 1,1–15, Matthew 1,1–4,16, Luke 1,1–4,30, John 1,1–15: The Gospel Prologues and Their Function." *Studia Evangelica* VI, 154–88. Berlin: Akademie, 1973.
Giblin, Charles H. "Reflections on the Sign of the Manger." *CBQ* 29 (1967) 87–101.
Gill, Christopher. "The Êthos/Pathos Distinction in Rhetorical and Literary Criticism." *CQ* 34 (1984) 149–66.
Gill, Christopher et al., eds. *Reciprocity in Ancient Greece.* Oxford: Clarendon, 1998.
Gilmore, David D., ed. *Honor and Shame and the Unity of the Mediterranean.* Special Publication of the American Anthropological Association 22. Washington, DC: American Anthropological Association, 1987.
Golden, Michael. "*Pais*, 'Child,' and 'Slave.'" *L'Antiquité Classique* 54 (1985) 91–104.
Goldin, Judah. "Not by Means of an Angel and not by Means of a Messenger." In *Religions in Antiquity: Essays in Memory of Erwin Ramsdell Goodenough*, edited by Jacob Neusner, 412–24. Studies in the History of Religion 14. Leiden: Brill, 1968.

Bibliography

Gouldner, Alvin W. "The Norm of Reciprocity: A Preliminary Statement." *American Sociological Review* 25 (1960) 161–78.
Guelich, Robert A. "The Beginning of the Gospel: Mark 1:1–15." *BR* 27 (1982) 5–15.
Green, Joel B. "The Problem of a Beginning: Israel's Scriptures in Luke 1–2." *BBR* 4 (1994) 61–85.
Grimes, Ronald L. "Defining Nascent Ritual." *JAAR* 50 (1982) 539–55.
Guijarro, Santiago. "The Politics of Exorcism." In *The Social Setting of Jesus and the Gospels*, edited by Wolfgang Stegemann et al., 159–74. Minneapolis: Fortress, 2002.
Habel, Norman C. "The Form and Significance of the Call Narrative." *ZAW* 77 (1965) 297–323.
Hanson, John. "Dreams and Visions in the Graeco-Roman World and Early Christianity." In *ANRW* II.23.2 (1980) 1395–427.
Hanson, K. C., and Douglas E. Oakman. *Palestine in the Time of Jesus: Social Structures and Social Conflicts*. 1st ed. Minneapolis: Fortress, 1998.
———. *Palestine in the Time of Jesus: Social Structures and Social Conflicts*. 2nd ed. Minneapolis: Fortress, 2008.
Harris, Elizabeth. *Prologue and Gospel: The Theology of the Fourth Evangelist*. JSNTSup 107. Sheffield: Sheffield Academic, 1994.
Harvey, A. E. "Son of God: The Constraints of Monotheism." In *Jesus and the Constraints of History*, 154–77. Philadelphia: Westminster, 1982.
Hermogenes. "The Preliminary Exercises Attributed to Hermogenes" In *Progymnasmata: Greek Textbooks of Prose Composition and Rhetoric*, translated by George A. Kennedy, 73–88. WGRW 10. Atlanta: SBL, 2003.
Hicks, R. D., trans. *Lives of Eminent Philosophers*, by Diogenes Laertius. Vol. 1. 2 vols. LCL. Cambridge: Harvard University Press, 1925.
Hill, David. "Rejection of Jesus at Nazareth (Luke 4:16–30)." *NovT* 13 (1971) 161–80.
Hock, Ronald F., trans. and ed. *The* Chreia *in Ancient Rhetoric: Commentaries on Aphthonius' Progymnasmata*. WGRW 31. Atlanta: SBL, 2012.
Hollenbach, Paul W. "The Conversion of Jesus: From Jesus the Baptizer to Jesus the Healer." In *ANRW* II.25.1 (1982) 196–219.
———. "Jesus, Demoniacs, and Public Authorities: A Social-Historical Study." *JAAR* 49 (1981) 561–88.
Hooker, Morna D. "John the Baptist and the Johannine Prologue." *NTS* 16 (1970) 354–58.
———. "The Johannine Prologue and the Messianic Secret." *NTS* 21 (1974) 40–58.
Hubbard, Benjamin J. "Commissioning Stories in Luke–Acts: Their Antecedents, Form and Content." *Semeia* 8 (1977) 103–26.
———. *The Matthean Redaction of a Primitive Apostolic Commissioning*. SBLDS 19. Missoula, MT: Scholars, 1974.
Husser, Jean-Marie. *Dreams and Dream Narratives in the Biblical World*. Biblical Seminar 63. Sheffield: Sheffield Academic, 1999.
Johnson, Luke T. *The Gospel of Luke*. SP 3. Collegeville, MN: Liturgical, 1991.
Jonge, H. J. de. "Sonship, Wisdom, Infancy: Luke ii.41–51a." *NTS* 24 (1978) 317–54.
Jonge, M. de. "The Use of the Word 'Anointed' in the Time of Jesus." *NovT* 8 (1966) 132–48.
Keck, Leander E. "The Introduction to Mark's Gospel." *NTS* 12 (1966) 252–70.
Kelber, Werner H. "The Birth of a Beginning: John 1:18." *Semeia* 52 (1990) 120–44.
Kennedy, George A., trans. *Progymnasmata: Greek Textbooks of Prose Composition and Rhetoric*. WGRW 10. Atlanta: SBL, 2003.

Bibliography

Lamour, David H. J. "Making Parallels: *Synkrisis* and Plutarch's 'Themistocles and Camillus.'" In *ANRW* II.33.6 (1991) 4154–204.

Lausberg, Heinrich. *Handbook of Literary Rhetoric: A Foundation for Literary Study.* Translated by Matthew T. Bliss et al. Edited by David E. Orton and R. Dean Anderson. Leiden: Brill, 1998.

LeClerc, Ivor, *Whitehead's Metaphysics: An Introductory Exposition.* New York: Macmillan, 1958.

Lund, Nils Wilhelm. *Chiasmus in the New Testament: A Study in Formgeschichte.* Chapel Hill: University of North Carolina Press, 1942.

———. "The Influence of Chiasmus on the Structure of the Gospel according to Matthew." *ATR* 13 (1931) 405–33.

———. "The Influence of Chiasmus on the Structure of the Gospels." *ATR* 13 (1931) 27–48.

Mack, Burton L., and Vernon K. Robbins. *Patterns of Persuasion in the Gospels.* Foundations & Facets: Literary Facets. 1989. Reprint, Eugene, OR: Wipf & Stock, 2008.

Malina, Bruce J. "Apocalyptic and Territoriality." In *Early Christianity in Context: Monuments and Documents; Essays in Honour of Emmanuel Testa,* edited by Fredrick Manns and Eugenio Alliata, 369–80. Studium Biblicum Franciscanum 38. Jerusalem: Franciscan, 1993.

———. *Christian Origins and Cultural Anthropology: Practical Models for Biblical Interpretation.* 1986. Reprint, Eugene, OR: Wipf & Stock, 2010.

———. "Dealing with Biblical (Mediterranean) Characters: A Guide for U.S. Consumers." *BTB* 19 (1989) 127–41.

———. *The New Testament World: Insights from Cultural Anthropology.* 3rd ed. Louisville: Westminster John Knox, 2001.

———. *On the Genre and Message of Revelation: Star Visions and Sky Journeys.* Peabody, MA: Hendrickson, 1995.

———. "Patron and Client: The Analogy behind Synoptic Theology." In *The Social World of Jesus and the Gospels,* 143–75. London: Routledge, 1996.

———. "Wealth and Poverty in the New Testament and Its World." *Int* 41 (1987) 354–67.

Malina, Bruce J., and Jerome H. Neyrey. *Calling Jesus Names: The Social Value of Labels in Matthew.* Foundations & Facets: Social Facets. Sonoma, CA: Polebridge, 1988.

———. "First-Century Personality: Dyadic, not Individualistic." In *The Social World of Luke–Acts: Models for Interpretation,* edited by Jerome H. Neyrey, 67–96. Peabody, MA: Hendrickson, 1991.

———. "Honor and Shame in Luke–Acts." In *The Social World of Luke–Acts: Models for Interpretation,* edited by Jerome H. Neyrey, 25–65. Peabody, MA: Hendrickson, 1991.

———. *Portraits of Paul: An Archaeology of Ancient Personality.* Louisville: Westminster John Knox, 1996.

Marcus, Joel. "Jesus' Baptismal Vision." *NTS* 41 (1995) 512–21.

Martin, Michael Wade. "The Encomiastic Topic of Syncrisis as the Key to the Structure and Argument of Hebrews." *NTS* 57 (2011) 415–39.

———."Philo's Use of Syncrisis: An Examination of Philonic Composition in the Light of the Progymnasmata." *PRS* 30 (2003) 271–97.

———. "Progymnastic Topic Lists: A Compositional Template for Luke and Other *Bioi*." *NTS* 54 (2008) 18–41.

Bibliography

Martin, Michael Wade, and Jason A. Whitlark. "Choosing What Is Advantageous: The Relationship between Epideictic and Deliberative Syncrisis in Hebrews." NTS 58 (2012) 379–400.

———. *Inventing Hebrews: Design and Purpose in Ancient Rhetoric.* SNTSMS 171. Cambridge: Cambridge University Press, 2018.

Matera, Frank J. "The Prologue as the Interpretative Key to Mark's Gospel." JSNT 34 (1988) 3–20.

McVann, Mark. "Ritual of Status Transformation in Luke–Acts: The Case of Jesus the Prophet." In *The Social World of Luke–Acts: Models for Interpretation*, edited by Jerome H. Neyrey, 333–60. Peabody, MA: Hendrickson, 1991.

Meeks, Wayne A. *The First Urban Christians: The Social World of the Apostle Paul.* New Haven: Yale University Press, 1983.

———. "Galilee and Judea in the Fourth Gospel." JBL 85 (1963) 159–69.

———. "The Man from Heaven in Johannine Sectarianism." JBL 91 (1972) 44–72.

Meynet, Roland. *Luke: The Gospel of the Children of Israel.* Retorica biblica e semitica 4. Rome: Gregorian & Biblical Press, 2015.

Minear, Paul S. "Dear Theo: The Kerygmatic Intention and the Claim of the Book of Acts." Int 27 (1973) 131–50.

Moessner, David P. "The Appeal and Power of Poetics (Luke 1:1–4): Luke's Superior Credentials (*Parēkolouthēkoti*), Narrative Sequence (*Kathexēs*), and Firmness of Understanding (*Hē Asphaleia*) for the Reader." In *Jesus and the Heritage of Israel: Luke's Narrative Claim upon Israel's Legacy*, 84–123. Harrisburg, PA: Trinity, 1999.

———. "'Eyewitnesses,' 'Informed Contemporaries,' and 'Unknowing Inquirers': Josephus' Criteria for Authentic Historiography and the Meaning of PARAKLOUTHEŌ." NovT 39 (1996) 105–22.

———. "The Triadic Synergy of Hellenistic Poetics in the Narrative Epistemology of Dionysius of Halicarnassus and the Authorial Intent of the Evangelist Luke (Luke 1:1–4; Acts 1:1–8)." Neotestamentica 42 (2008) 289–303.

Mowrey, Robert L. "The Divine Hand and the Divine Plan in the Lukan Passion." In SBLSP 1991, 558–75.

———. "Lord, God, and Father: Theological Language in Luke–Acts." In SBLSP 1995, 82–101.

Moxnes, Halvor. "Honor and Shame." In *The Social Sciences and New Testament Interpretation*, edited by Richard L. Rohrbaugh, 19–40. Peabody, MA: Hendrickson, 1996.

Mullins, Terrence Y. "The New Testament Commission Form, Especially in Luke–Acts." JBL 95 (1976) 603–14.

Nepos, Cornelius. *De Viris Illustribus, Epamonidas.* In *Cornelius Nepos.* Translated by John C. Rolfe. LCL. Cambridge: Harvard University Press, 1984.

Neyrey, Jerome H. *An Encomium for Jesus: Luke, Rhetoric and the Story of Jesus.* New Testament Monographs 40. Sheffield: Sheffield Phoenix, 2020.

———. "Encomium versus Vituperation: Contrasting Portraits of Jesus in the Fourth Gospel." JBL 126 (2007) 529–52.

———. "'First,' 'Only,' 'One of a Few,' and 'No One Else': The Rhetoric of Uniqueness and the Doxologies in 1 Timothy." Bib 86 (2005) 59–87.

———. "The Foot Washing in John 13:6–11: Transformation Ritual or Ceremony?" In *The Social World of the First Christians: Essays in Honor of Wayne A. Meeks*, edited by Michael White and O. Larry Yarbrough, 198–213. Minneapolis: Fortress, 1995.

Bibliography

———. *The Gospel of John*. New Cambridge Bible Commentary. Cambridge: Cambridge University Press, 2007.

———. *Honor and Shame in the Gospel of Matthew*. Louisville: Westminster John Knox, 1998.

———. "I Said: 'You are Gods': Psalm 82 and John 10." *JBL* 108 (1989) 655–59.

———. "'How Does This Man Have Learning, Since He Is without Education?' (John 7:15)." *BTB* 48 (2018) 85–96.

———. "Jesus, Gender and the Gospel of Matthew." *Semeia* 45 (2003) 43–66.

———. "Lost in Translation: Did It Matter If Christians 'Thanked' God or 'Gave God Glory'?" *CBQ* 71 (2009) 1–23.

———. "The 'Noble Shepherd' in John 10: Cultural and Rhetorical Background." *JBL* 120 (2001) 267–91.

———. *Paul, in Other Words: A Cultural Reading of His Letters*. Louisville: Westminster John Knox, 1990.

———. *The Passion according to Luke: A Redaction Study of Luke's Soteriology*. Theological Inquiries. New York: Paulist, 1985.

———. "Questions, *Chreiai*, and Challenges to Honor. The Interface of Rhetoric and Culture in Mark's Gospel." *CBQ* 60 (1998) 657–81.

———, ed. *The Social World of Luke–Acts: Models for Interpretation*. Peabody, MA: Hendrickson, 1991.

———. "Spaces and Places, Whence and Whither, Homes and Rooms: 'Territoriality' in the Fourth Gospel." *BTB* 32 (2002) 60–74.

———. "The Symbolic Universe of Luke–Acts: 'They Turn the World Upside Down.'" In *The Social World of Luke–Acts: Models for Interpretation*, 271–304. Peabody, MA: Hendrickson, 1991.

———. "Syncrisis and Encomium: Reading Hebrews through Greek Rhetoric." *CBQ* 82 (2020) 276–99.

Neyrey, Jerome H., and Richard L. Rohrbaugh. "'He Must Increase, I Must Decrease' (John 3:30): A Cultural and Social Interpretation." *CBQ* 63 (2001) 464–83.

Nolland, John. *Luke 1—9:20*. Word Biblical Commentary 35A. Dallas: Word, 1989.

Oakman, Douglas, E. *Jesus and the Peasants*. Matrix: The Bible in Mediterranean Context 4. Eugene, OR: Cascade Books, 2008.

———. *The Political Aims of Jesus*. Minneapolis: Fortress, 2012.

O'Fearghail, Fearghus. *The Introduction to Luke–Acts: A Study of the Role of Luke 1,1—4,44 in the Composition of Luke's Two-Volume Work*. Analecta biblica 126. Rome: Pontifical Biblical Institute Press, 1991.

———. "The Literary Forms of Lk 1,5–25 and 1,26–39." *Marianum* 43 (1981) 321–44.

———. "Rejection in Nazareth: Lk 4:22." *ZNW* 75 (1984) 60–72.

O'Hair, Dan, et al. *A Speaker's Guidebook: Text and Reference*. Boston: Bedford/St. Martin's, 2012.

O'Toole, Robert, "Parallels between Jesus and His Disciples in Luke–Acts: A Further Study." *BZ* 27 (1983) 195–212.

Parsons, Mikeal C. *Luke*. Paedeia. Grand Rapids: Baker Academic, 2015.

———. *Luke: Storyteller, Interpreter, Evangelist*. Peabody, MA: Hendrickson, 2007.

Parsons, Mikeal C., and Michael Wade Martin. *Ancient Rhetoric and the New Testament*. Waco: Baylor University Press, 2018.

Peristiany, J. G., ed. *Honour and Shame: The Values of Mediterranean Society*. The Nature of Human Society Series. Chicago: University of Chicago Press, 1966.

BIBLIOGRAPHY

Peristiany, J. G., and Julian Pitt-Rivers, eds. *Honor and Grace in Anthropology*. Studies in Social and Cultural Anthropology 76. Cambridge: Cambridge University Press, 1992.

Picirelli, Robert. "The Meaning of *Epignosis*." *EvQ* 47 (1975) 85–93.

Pilch, John J. "Altered States of Consciousness in the Synoptics." In *The Social Setting of Jesus and the Gospels*, edited by Wolfgang Stegemann et al., 103–15. Minneapolis: Fortress, 2002.

———. *A Cultural Handbook to the Bible*. Grand Rapids: Eerdmans, 2012.

Plato. *Menexenus*. In *Timaeus, Critias, Cleitophon, Menexenus, Epistles*. Translated by N. R. M. Lamb. LCL. Cambridge: Harvard University Press, 1960.

Plutarch. *Moralia*. Translated by Frank Cole Babbitt. LCL. Cambridge: Harvard University Press, 1949.

———. *On Love of Wealth*. In *Moralia*. Translated by Paul A. Clement. LCL. Cambridge: Harvard University Press, 1969.

———. *Plutarch's Lives*. Vol. 4, *Life of Alciabades*. Translated by Bernadotte Perrin. 11 vols. LCL. Cambridge: Harvard University Press, 1968.

———. *Table Talk*, vol. 5. In *Moralia*, Vol. 9. Translated by Edwin L. Minar et al. LCL. Cambridge: Harvard University Press, 1961.

Pokorný, Petr. "Anfang des Evangeliums: Zur Problem des Anfangs und des Schlusses des Markusevangeliums." In *Die Kirche des Anfangs: Festschrift für Heinz Schürmann zum 65. Geburtstag*, edited by Rudolf Schnackenburg et al., 115–31. Erfurter theologische Studien 38. Leipzig: St. Benno, 1977.

Quintilian. *Institutio Oratoriae*. Translated by Donald Russell. LCL. Cambridge: Harvard University Press, 2001.

Reese, James M. "The Principal Model of God in the New Testament." *BTB* 8 (1978) 126–31.

Robinson, J. A. T. "The Baptism of John and the Qumran Community." *HTR* 50 (1957) 175–91.

———. "The Relation of the Prologue to the Gospel of St. John." *NTS* 9 (1963) 120–29.

Robbins, Vernon K. "Prefaces in Greco-Roman Biography and Luke–Acts." *PRSt* 6 (1979) 94–108.

Rohrbaugh, Richard L. "Ethnocentrism and Historical Questions about Jesus." In *The Social Setting of Jesus and the Gospels*, edited by Wolfgang Stegemann et al., 27–42. Minneapolis: Fortress, 2002.

———. "Gossip in the New Testament." In *Social Scientific Models for Interpreting the Bible: Essays by the Context Group in Honor of Bruce J. Malina*, edited by John J. Pilch, 236–59. BibIntSer 53. Leiden: Brill, 2000.

———. "Legitimating Sonship—A Test of Honour: A Social-Scientific Study of Luke 4:1–30." In *Modelling Early Christianity: Social-Scientific Studies in the New Testament and Its Context*, edited by Philip F. Esler, 183–97. London: Routledge, 1994.

———. "Luke's Jesus: Honor Claimed, Honor Tested." In *The New Testament in Cross-Cultural Perspective*, 31–44. Matrix: The Bible in Mediterranean Context 1. Eugene, OR: Cascade Books, 2007.

———. *The New Testament in Cross-Cultural Perspective*. Matrix: The Bible in Mediterranean Context 1. Eugene, OR: Cascade Books, 2007.

———. "The Social Function of Genealogies in the New Testament and Its World." In *To Set at Liberty: Essays on Early Christianity and Its Social World in Honor of John H.*

Bibliography

Elliott, edited by Stephen K. Black, 311–27. The Social World of Biblical Antiquity 2nd ser., 11. Sheffield: Sheffield Phoenix, 2014.

———. "The Social Location of the Markan Audience." *BTB* 23 (1993) 114–27.

Rothwell, J. Dan. *In the Company of Others: An Introduction to Communication*. 3rd ed. New York: Oxford University Press, 2010.

Russell, D. A. "On Reading Plutarch's *Lives*." *Greece and Rome* 13 (1966) 139–54.

Russell, D. A., and N. G. Wilson, eds. and trans. *Menander Rhetor*. Oxford: Clarendon, 1981.

Saburin, Richard A. "The Growing of Christ: Understanding Luke 2:40, 52 in the Light of Structural Pattern of Luke–Acts." *Journal of Asia Adventist Seminary* 10 (2007) 15–25.

Sahlins, Marshall. *Stone Age Economics*. Chicago: Alderline-Atherton, 1973.

Said, Edward. *Beginnings: Intention and Method*. New York: Basic Books, 1975.

Schneider, Gerhard. "Zur Bedeutung von καθεξῆς im lukanischen Doppelwerk." *ZNW* 68 (1977) 128–31.

Schwartz, Shalom H. "Individualism–Collectivism: Critique and Proposed Refinements." *Journal of Cross-Cultural Psychology* 21 (1990) 139–57.

Seitz, Oscar J. F. "Gospel Prologues: A Common Pattern?" *JBL* 83 (1964) 262–68.

Skorupski, John. *Symbol and Theory: A Philosophical Study of Theories of Religion in Social Anthropology*. Cambridge: Cambridge University Press, 1976.

Squires, John T. *The Plan of God in Luke–Acts*. SNTSMS 76. Cambridge: Cambridge University Press, 1993.

Stadter, P. A. "Plutarch's Comparison of Pericles and Fabius Maximus." *GRBS* 16 (1975) 77–85.

Stansell, Gary. "The Gift in Ancient Israel." *Semeia* 87 (2006) 65–90.

———. "Gifts, Tribute, and Offerings." In *The Social Setting of Jesus and the Gospels*, edited by Wolfgang Stegemann et al., 349–67. Minneapolis: Fortress, 2002.

Stendahl, Krister. "*Quis et Unde*? An Analysis of Mt 1–2." In *Judentum Urchristentum Kirche: Festschrift für Joachim Jeremias*, edited by Walter Eltester, 94–105. Berlin: Töpelmann, 1964.

Stevenson, T. R. "The Ideal Benefactor and the Father Analogy in Greek and Roman Thought." *CQ* 42 (1992) 421–36.

Talbert, Charles H. "Prophecies of Future Greatness: The Contribution of Greco-Roman Biographies to an Understanding of Luke 1:5—4:15." In *The Divine Helmsman: Studies on God's Control of Human Events Presented to Lou H. Silberman*, edited by James L. Crenshaw and Samuel Sandmel, 136–37. New York: Ktav, 1980.

Theon, Aelius. *The Exercises of Aelius Theon*. In *Progymnasmata: Greek Textbooks of Prose Composition and Rhetoric*, translated by George A. Kennedy, 3–72. WGRW 10. Atlanta: SBL, 2003.

Thompson, G. H. P. "Called—Proved—Obedient: A Study in the Baptism and Temptation Narratives of Matthew and Luke." *JTS* n.s. 11 (1960) 1–12.

Thompson, Marianne Meye. "'God's Voice You Have not Heard, God's Form You Have never Seen': Characterization of God in the Gospel of John." *Semeia* 63 (1993) 177–205.

Triandis, Harry C. "Cross-Cultural Studies in Individualism and Collectivism." In *Cross-Cultural Perspectives*, edited by John J. Berman, 41–133. Nebraska Symposium on Motivation 37. Lincoln: University of Nebraska Press, 1990.

BIBLIOGRAPHY

———. *Individualism and Collectivism*. New Directions in Social Psychology. Boulder, CO: Westview, 1995.
Turner, Victor, *The Forest of Symbols: Aspects of Ndembu Ritual*. Ithaca, NY: Cornell University Press, 1967.
Uro, Risto. "Ritual and Christian Origins." In *Understanding the Social World of the New Testament*, edited by Dietmar Neufeld and Richard E. DeMaris, 120–32. London: Routledge, 2010.
Unnik, W. C. van. "Once More St. Luke's Prologue." *Neotestamentica* 9 (1973) 7–26.
———. *Tarsus or Jerusalem, the City of Paul's Youth*. Translated by George Ogg. London: Epworth, 1962.
Wees, Hans van. ""Reciprocity in Anthropological Theory." In *Reciprocity in Ancient Greece*, edited by Christopher Gill et al., 13–50. Oxford: Oxford University Press, 1998.
Wills, Lawrence. "The Form of the Sermon in Hellenistic Judaism and Early Christianity." *HTR* 1977 (1984) 277–99.
Wisse, Jakob. *Ethos and Pathos from Aristotle to Cicero*. Amsterdam: Hakkert, 1989.
Xenophon. *Hiero*. In *Scripta Minora*. Translated by E. C. Marchant. Xenophon in 7 vols., 6. LCL. Cambridge: Harvard University Press, 1918.
———. *Memorabilia*. In *Memorabilia* and *Oeconomicus*. Translated by E. C. Marchant. Xenophon in 7 vols., 4. LCL. Cambridge: Harvard University Press, 1918.
York, John O. *The Last Shall Be First: The Rhetoric of Reversal in Luke*. JSNTSup 46. Sheffield: JSOT Press, 1991.

Index of Subjects

Abraham, 23–24, 47, 84–85, 102
Aelius Theon, 104, 122
angels as channels, 1, 9–11, 13, 30, 34, 46
Anna, 15, 32, 94
Aphthonius, 103–4, 121
Aristotle
   Rhetoric
      Book One, 12, 24, 25, 27–29, 111, 113, 114, 116, 121, 122
      Book Two, 25, 27, 101, 111, 113, 122
      Book Three, 25, 28, 78, 79, 80, 111, 118
   Virtues and Vices, 114

beginning(s), 22–23, 77–99, 111–12
   ethos created, 77, 81–99, 111–12, 130
   encomium topics, 81–83, 89–92, 101–2
   exordium, 25–26, 78–81, 111–12
   preface, 88–89, 116–20

challenge/riposte, 55, 58, 61, 67, 69–70, 73
   see questions
ceremonies,
   see ritual
chreia, 40, 55–59, 61, 63, 66–74
Cicero
   Inv. 19, 80–81, 119
   Orat. 54–55, 56, 91, 104–5, 120, 122, 126, 128
communication, direct, 19, 20, 24, 30, 50

communications model, 8–30, 34, 46, 50, 83, 85–87, 94, 100, 106–8, 109, 128–29
   Aristotle and, 24–28
   classicists and, 28–30
   sender/speaker, 25, 28–29
   channel/receiver, 25–27, 29
   message/logos, 26–29
   purpose, 28, 31
commissioning model, 106–8
conflict,
   see challenge/riposte, chreia
context, high and low, 12, 60–61

Elizabeth, 11, 15
encomium, 17–18, 81–83, 96, 101–4
   origins, 16, 18, 32, 33–34, 46–47, 84–86, 89–91, 93–94, 98, 102
   nurture/training, 18, 83–84, 87–88, 91–92, 95–97, 98, 102–3, 109
ethos
   rhetorical discussion of, 29–30, 35, 77, 81, 82, 99, 100–103
   of Jesus, 9, 12, 21, 32, 36, 42–50, 82–88, 100–109
   of John, 16–17, 87–88
   of Luke, 110–28
   a proper ethos, 112–15, 115–20
ethos, three conventional topics
   wise, 113–14, 116–18
   virtuous/benevolent, 114–15, 118–20
   courageous, 115–16, 120–22

Index of Subjects

God, 22–24
    anoints Jesus, 20–21, 50
    ascribes honor, 10–13, 39, 40,
        49–50
    creates ethos for Jesus, 12
    Father, 34–35, 37
    plan and purpose of, 10, 22–24,
        33, 37, 41, 47
    Sender-of-Senders, 9–15, 16–17,
        22–24, 34, 46, 109
group-oriented person, 33–37, 41
    honor and shame orientation,
        37–40
    Jesus as, 33–37
    obedience, 34–35
    socialization, *see below*

Herrenium, Rhetorica ad, 113, 119,
    127, 128
holy spirit, 11, 14, 16, 20, 21, 49
honor, pivotal value, 7, 9, 12–13, 20,
    31, 32–40, 45, 109, 115–16,
    122, 125
Jesus
    ascribed honor of, 10–13, 39, 40,
        49–50
    anointed by God, 20–21, 50
    beloved son, 11–12, 23, 30,
        33–35, 42, 49
    Christ the Lord, 12, 23, 27, 39, 46
    ethos of, 9, 12, 21, 32, 36, 42–50,
        82–88, 100–109
    honor of, 6, 11–12, 22–23, 31, 36,
        39, 55–56
    holy one of God, 27, 41–42
    Logos, 51–53
    names of, 52, 67–69
    obedience of, 22, 33, 34, 37, 53,
        56, 58
    prophet, 36–37
    reputation of, 35–36, 38, 39, 42
    roles and statuses of, *see below*
    son of David, 30, 41, 52, 54
    son of God, 30, 34–35, 57–58
    son of the Most High, 23, 24,
        30, 34

    syncrisis with John, 10–11,
        104–5, 107
    teacher, 1–2, 59–60, 66–67
John the Baptist, 15–19, 32, 83–84
John the Evangelist, 88–92
Joseph, 10, 13, 15, 46, 62

kinship, 33–34, 37, 41, 51, 93

limited good, 61–62
Luke, 2, 63, 66, 116–29

Mark, 83–84
Mary, 1, 11–12, 13, 15, 47, 104–5
Matthew, 84–88
Menander Rhetor, 87n20, 118n21

names, 52, 67–70
Nepos
    Epam., 101

Passover, 54–56
patron-client model, 67–70
person, ancient vs modern, 35–36
person, group-oriented, 1, 32–37, 95
Plutarch
    Alcibiedes, 38
    Love of Wealth, 39
    Moralia, 109
    Table Talk, 38, 39
progymnasmata, 3, 80–81, 108–9
    see chreia, encomium, syncrisis
prologue/preface, 88–89, 110–15,
    116–20
prominence, 45–49
prophecy-fulfilment, 11, 14, 17, 21,
    22–24, 86
public voice, 7–9, 16, 41, passim

questions, 55, 58, 67, 73
    see challenge and riposte
Quintilian
    Inst.Orat., 32, 38, 80, 122

ritual, elements of
    frequency, 43, 49, 52, 54, 59, 60
    calendar, 44, 49, 54, 56, 59, 60, 72

Index of Subjects

temporal focus, 44, 49, 55, 57, 60
presider, 44, 49, 52, 56, 60–61
purpose, 44, 48–49, 50, 52, 56, 57, 61
ritual, confirming ceremony, 44, 54–71, 72–74
  synagogue meeting as, 63–66, 71–72
ritual, status elevation, 43, 45–50
ritual, types of, 42–45, 46, 52–53
ritualized combat, 49, 51–52, 61–63, 64–66, 71–73
  as regular part of synagogue ritual, 64–65
  see chreia
role and status, 7, 9, 10–11, 13, 14, 20, 30, 40–45, 50, 51–52, 72, 107–8

sabbath, 54, 59, 60–61, 63–65, 66–67, 72
signs, as proof, 11–12, 13, 29
Simeon, 14–15, 94
socialization, 95–97, 102–3
stereotypes, 33, 36, 59, 87–88, 110, 129
synagogue meeting, typical elements of, 63–66, 72
syncrisis, 18, 83–84, 96–97, 98, 103, 106–8, 119, 122–26, 130

Zechariah, 11–12, 15–16, 24, 32, 104–5

Index of Scripture

HEBREW BIBLE

Genesis
3	56

Exodus
7:3	11
13:1–2	49
20:8–11	72
20:18–19	30

Deuteronomy
4:34	11
5:12–15	72
16:16	55
23:2	32

2 Kings
9:22	32

Job
11:7–9	89

Psalms
78:43	11
105:27	11

Isaiah
40:3	83
57:3	32
61:1	60, 64

Ezekiel
16:44	32

Micah
5:2	86

APOCRYPHA

Sirach
23:25–26	32
30:7	32

NEW TESTAMENT

Matthew
1:1	84, 85
1:2–17	84
1:19–20	85, 86
1:21	85
2:1–12	82
2:2	47, 85
2:5	86
2:6	82
2:12–13	86
3:2	84
4:24–25	88
4:32	88
11:27	32
24:24	11

Index of Scripture

Mark

1:1–5	68
1:2–3	83
1:4–6	83
1:7–8	83
1:9	83
1:10–11	83
1:14–15	84
1:44	44
6:3	18
13:22	11

Luke

1:1–4	78, 100–131
1:5–20	65, 106, 107
1:5	16, 32
1:20	82
1:22	12
1:26–39	105–7
1:27	32, 93
1:30–36	10–13, 34, 37
1:30	10
1:31–33	36, 47
1:32	10, 21, 40
1:33	10
1:35	11, 21, 40, 59
1:36	11
1:37	12
1:54	24, 47
1:55	47
1:64	16
1:66	16
1:68	16
1:72–73	23, 47
1:76	16, 17
2:4	34, 93
2:6–7	45
2:7–9	32
2:10–11	13, 102
2:11–18	13–14
2:11	12, 34, 40, 47, 93
2:12	11, 12, 37
2:13–14	12
2:16	12
2:17	12, 46
2:18	12
2:21	45, 68
2:22	94
2:24	94
2:25–38	14–15, 46
2:25	14, 27, 57, 95
2:26	14, 57, 94
2:28	47, 94
2:30–32	14, 37
2:30	14, 47, 94
2:32	14
2:37	15
2:38	15, 94
2:41–52	45, 54–56
2:41	55, 95
2:46	94, 95
2:47	34
2:49	37
2:51	34, 37, 55, 56, 96, 97, 102
3:1–17	15–20
3:1–15	88
3:2	17, 32, 87, 88
3:3	16, 84
3:4	17
3:5	87
3:6	87
3:7–10	87, 88
3:9	19
3:11	88
3:13	87
3:14–15	87
3:15–17	19
3:15	16, 17
3:16	19, 57
3:17	19
3:20	108
3:21–22	20–22, 24, 34, 37, 45, 49–50, 56, 72, 100, 108
3:21	57
3:22	20, 46
3:23–38	34, 82
4:1–13	37, 54, 56–50, 66, 67
4:13	67
4:14–15	2, 38, 56–60
4:15	1, 2
4:15–16	54, 95

Index of Scripture

4:16–30	2, 36, 60–63, 64, 66	11:17–22	57, 71
4:17–20	54, 74	11:24	57
4:17	88	11:42–52	36
4:22	62	11:43	64
4:23	61, 66	13:11	57
4:24	62	13:32	69
4:29	62	14:28–32	9
4:31–37	54, 66–71	17:13	68
4:31	1, 66	18:13–14	44
4:32	66	18:37–38	33, 68
4:33	57, 66	20:2	1
4:34	33, 66, 67, 68, 69	20:21	70
4:36–37	71	20:27	33, 36
4:37	38	22:3	67
4:41	67	22:31	67
4:43	37	22:44	49
5:10	34	22:54–62	56
5:15	38	23:3	67
5:17	33	23:35–37	56
5:25–26	38	23:42	68
6:1–5	74		
6:5	73	**John**	
6:6–11	72, 73–74	1:1–18	78, 88–92
6:6	73	1:2	90
6:7	73	1:4	92
6:10	74	1:5	92
6:15–16	32	1:9	92
6:18	57	1.10–11	92
7:17	38	1:12	92
7:18–23	108	1:14	90, 92
7:19	17	1:18	89, 92
7:20	19	1:45	90, 91
7:21	57	1:46	82, 102
7:28	19	1:49	91
8:2	57	1:51	91
8:19–20	37	2:11	11
8:21	37	3:12	92
8:27–38	67	3:30	19
8:28	68	6:42	91
8:39	38	6:62	96
8:49	64	7:27–28	90
9:1	67	7:41	91
9:18–20	37	8:14	90
9:42	57, 67	8:23	90
10:13	37	9:29–30	90
10:17	67		
11:8–13	69		

Index of Scripture

Acts of the Apostles

2:3	49
2:22	11
2:32–36	40
2:33	21, 39
2:36	21, 39
2:43	11
4:13	97
4:16	11
6:9	64
7:2–8	23
7:36	11
9:2	65
13:15	64
13:32–33	24
17:3	65
17:9	65
18:4	65
18:8	64
19:8	65
21:39	82
22:3	97
22:19	65
24:12	95

Romans

13:1	33

1 Corinthians

7:5	65
12:18	33

2 Corinthians

11:24–25	65

Galatians

6:1	56

Philippians

2:10	89
3:5	97

www.ingramcontent.com/pod-product-compliance
Lightning Source LLC
Chambersburg PA
CBHW022120160426
43197CB00009B/1102